3rd Advanced Architecture Contest

SELF
SUFFICIENT
CITY

Envisioning the habitat of the future

organized by

GW00392198

in collaboration with

A NEW CHALLENGE
Beatriz Corredor, Minister of Housing

The competition 'The Self-sufficient City' has stimulated a worldwide debate on the future of our cities. In the wake of the previous competitions 'Self-sufficient Housing' and 'The Self-Fab House', on this occasion the Institute for Advanced Architecture of Catalonia is inviting reflection on how we will live in the near future in the light of the social, cultural and technological changes in which we are immersed. The involvement of more than 700 participants, mostly architects and architecture students, from over 100 countries, reflects the very great interest in the design of the future of our cities, especially among young people.

Throughout its history Spain has created some of the finest examples of architecture and urban space rich in qualities that have contributed to the social and economic progress of its citizens. In 1859, the Cerdá Plan for Barcelona marked a turning point in the history of what has come to be known urbanism, putting forward a rational system of inhabiting the territory, responding effectively to the social needs of the time and anticipating the importance of mobility and infrastructure in the modern city. Spain's transition to democracy in the last quarter of the 20th century was also of crucial significance in its renewed commitment to the urban space: all across the country there were major transformations in the upgrading of infrastructure and the renewal of neighbourhoods, the construction of facilities and the design of public spaces. And now the 21st century presents us with the challenge of sustainability and the rehabilitation of our neighbourhoods and cities in such a way as to define new models of energy efficiency that will enable us to face the future of our cities with optimism. In concluding I would like to congratulate the organizers of and the participants in the competition for their contribution to the debate on the future of urban culture, and encourage them to take part, through their projects and initiatives, in the transformation of their cities in order to define a future at both the local and the global level that will promote sustainable development.

SALVE, CITIZEN
Javier Nieto, IaaC President

This twenty-first century will be the century of the cities. We know that by 2050 over 70% of the world's population will live in a city, as more than half of us already do, and that this will involve a paradigm shift in human history. In the information society, in which we have limitless access to data via the screens in our pockets, the territorial centralities which manifest themselves in our cities are the nodes that enable us to meet and interact person to person. The city thus affirms its strategic value as a geo-graphical focus in the territory, as a setting for communal life and sociability. More than ever the city will be culture: a space of freedom and contact, a space for creation and exchange. And the construction of just such a quality public space, at the human scale, with efficient energy-sustainable systems of mobility, where people are the essential core, is what today defines the value of a city and will do so even more in the immediate future.

At the IaaC we believe that harmony is to be achieved through the right interaction of three elements: people, city and planet. Human beings and their sphere of needs, real and aspirational, are the radical motive behind every work. The city, as the most specifically human of the phenomena that articulate the territory, is our closest ecosystem. And the planet, the home of all of us, as the scale that defines the limitations, in which natural flows and the infrastructures we make interact, is our inescapable frame of reference. From the global village to the open metapolis. And to make this possible design, architecture, urbanism and their associated disciplines must foster an excellence that seeks the proper balance between development and conservation.

The IaaC as an academic institution is committed to that excellence, and to stimulating the imagination and debate about the future of our cities. Therefore we warmly welcome the participation of all the teams that have submitted proposals to the competition, and open our doors to them in a spirit of sincere cooperation. *Salve*, citizen: we are ready to debate with you. We all have a huge task ahead of us.

CAN THE PLANET WITHSTAND ANOTHER 20TH CENTURY?
Vicente Guallart, IaaC Director

The architecture of the 21st century will be the first that is part of natural history. The machineries of consumption and appropriation of the environment and its resources are pushing the global habitat toward collapse from exhaustion. The direct consequence of an age in which economic growth inevitably entailed physical growth. Architecture and the city are the interface that we have provided ourselves with in order to interact with the world. At the local and the global scale.

Is it possible to define a general theory of multiscalar habitability on which we can live our lives in the decades to come?

We make the world fit for us to inhabit by means of functional nodes linked by networks that structure a once natural environment. A networked world.

Architecture is the functional precipitation of activities in a place.

Ordered crystals, condensers of micro worlds. Condensation of knowledge.

If recent history has been constructed on the basis of centralized systems of energy, information or production, the new history will be constructed on the basis of distributed, decentralized systems, by way of operational nodes —people, things, places, territories— that cooperate freely in order to be more efficient.

What is the architecture for distributed systems like?

As in all mutations, the saturation of the city's vital systems leads to their re-programming on the basis of principles that are closer to those of information systems than the simple accumulation of inorganic matter.

Time and, with it, speed serve to define the rhythm of interaction between people and their environment.

A new material in project design.

More ordered information creates a world that is more specific, not more generic.

A world capable of accumulating history inside itself.

What makes us human beings, not bacteria, is that our cells have managed to conserve information about their history through each mutation.

To construct anywhere on the planet is to submit the site to structural changes, which should be the product of the emerging relationships with the place, like a geological process of saturation or erosion.

More connected information generates more nature.

The re-programming of the world occurs when a fine informational rain is capable of drenching every element on the planet, endowing it with a digital identity, enabling it to interact with other elements by means of decentralized relational protocols.

In this way we create living organisms, never again inert, that react to specific geographies and mutate, where appropriate, in response to external influences.

Rather than being a client node in a network, then, architecture is an entity that tends toward the connected self-sufficiency characteristic of natural systems.

Buildings as trees. Cities as forests.

Are architects, architects of information architecture?

The citizens, instead of being the consumers of information, are its creators.

The citizens, instead of being the consumers of architecture, can be its constructors.

Is architecture an iconic or a systemic activity?

Finally, every object we design and construct on the planet forms part of a functional network that connects the different scales of habitability.

1, 10, 100, 1,000, 10,000, 100,000, 1,000,000, 10,000,000, 100,000,000, 1,000,000,000, 10,000,000,000 people organize themselves by programming their relationship with the other scales by way of relational systems whose structure defines the cultural values of each society. From a book to the Library of Congress; from a lamp to a nuclear power station; from a crucifix to the Vatican.

Any object, any building is ultimately the physical representation of an information node.

The construction of a dwelling, a block or a city is part of the same project of multiscalar habitability.

To change the history of the world is to change the history of the scalar relations between the functional networks of habitability.

Architecture can remain in the realm of fashion, as an activity that acts on the surface of things, or it can lead this structural transformation through which we can help to write a new history of the world.

Manifesto 11 Biennale di Venezia. July 2008

THE CITY AND ME

Willi Müller, IaaC Development Director

One of the most widely used resources in any critical appraisal of the future of the contemporary city always inevitably contains a vision of disaster, the final and foretold collapse, approached either explicitly or naively, addressing the consequences or lamenting them.

Film is — or was? — the most important visual format of our time, and unlike contemporary images, which are more concerned with explaining the effects of disasters on people or things than with their causes, it has been regularly supplying us with unforgettable sequences of that anticipated urban catastrophe for many decades, from Fritz Lang's *Metropolis* in the 20s to *Blade Runner* by Ridley Scott in the 80s, to name just two I wickedly enjoy. In this century the video game has prophetically — and I say this because it can be classed as entertainment but not as culture, making it a genuine reagent from a cultural point of view — come to occupy the visual space of urban catastrophe: *Urban Chaos* on PlayStation.

The original *Urban Chaos* was a project launched in 2000 by the British company Mucky Foot Productions. The game was a third-person action adventure which took place in an urban environment where shootouts and car chases were the key scenarios. The new version from Rocksteady Studios, *Riot Response* — the subtitle of the 2006 *Urban Chaos* — gives us a *first-person* game with a story line centred on street gangs and the battle-field that the city has become.

How did we get here?

Leaving aside the extensive body of more or less vision-ary fantasy literature about these processes, and of more or less abundant ideological writing, quite a number of texts from the 70s have had a considerable if unobtrusive influence on the approach that disciplines from sociology to town planning have taken to the urban phenomenon: in summary form, such texts have focused on the phe-nomena of breakdown and discontinuity, and we have been more or less repeatedly revising, extending or cor-recting them ever since when we analyse why our cities have been working for some time now with models of future collapse and projects to prevent it.

Everywhere in nature we find continuous changes that give rise to discontinuous leaps. This is what led René Thom to formulate catastrophe theory, a mathematical model which envisages a number of patterns of behav-iour in systems that experience a sudden change in structure as a result of continuous changes in the parameters which control that structure. This relation-ship between continuity and radical change can also be expressed very simply as 'the straw that broke the camel's back', the point at which the latest small incre-ment in an ongoing process causes the whole structure to collapse.

In other words, the process has undergone a *bifurca-tion*, which is what happens when a system changes from a stable to an unstable state, at which point it seeks to achieve stability again: a catastrophe is a bifurcation between two distinct stable states. Thom listed seven elementary catastrophes, each of which has a geometric representation determined by its respective mathemati-cal equation. He called these fold, cusp, swallowtail, butterfly, hyperbolic umbilic, elliptic umbilic and parabolic umbilic, according to the forms they took.

These theories, which were applied across the whole spectrum of dynamic systems — of which the city is one — were gradually reformulated, according to critics of this model, thanks to the Chaos theory pioneered by Edward Lorenz, essentially because this provided a more effective synthesis of the seven elementary catastrophes in a set of three concepts: fixed point, limit cycle and strange attractors — forces that operate on different wavelengths in the system and change its dynamics. Nowadays, when we are witnessing a parameterization of foreseeable models of behaviour at every possible scale, from design to the economy, the city still proves stubbornly intractable, a scenario where the dreams or nightmares of what could have been but never was linger on, seen in a positive or a negative light.

There is a good case for revising some of the thinking about urban behaviour in terms of models of analysis which can parameterize behaviour patterns, but from a new angle: the action has to be *first-person* It is as emotional actors in this game of belonging to a city, halfway between being a citizen and a tourist, that we can really take control of these attractors. The city must therefore be much more than an appropriate functional structure in which density, traffic, building regulations, mobility and all the other endlessly debated classic concepts are duly dealt with — that is to say discussed — and become part of a different community, an *emotional structure* lived in the first person, participatory, negotiable and real.

Chaos, then, is part of a bifurcation, a search for the first-hand experience of being part of the city as an alternative to being something at a given moment and becoming something else a moment later. The city and me.

IS IT POSSIBLE NOT ONLY T[O]
THE DEGRADATION CAUSED
FOR THE CITIES OF THE FUTU[RE]
WHICH CULTIVATES OUR SO[UL]

PROTECT THE PLANET FROM
OUR CITIES AT PRESENT, BUT
RE TO BECOME THE MEDIUM
S?

MIGHT OUR CITY MODE
BEHAVIORAL CHANGES C
NEOUSLY TO THE BETTEF
ENVIRONMENT?

BE RESPONSIVE TO OUR
VER TIME AND SIMULTA-
MENT OF THE URBAN

CAN WE CONCEIVE 'PLANNING' AND YE MINACY?

CITIES THROUGH
T RETAIN INDETER-

A WORLD OF SETTINGS
Lucas Cappelli, Director of Advanced Architecture Contest

In our daily interaction with the city we have, up until now, burdened ourselves with the tedious and repetitive task of opting. Opting for this or that, opting almost always for the same thing at the same time.

Our vehicle knows it has to start the engine when I get in, without my having to turn a key. It also knows that I will want to leave the place where I'm parked, and it knows that I don't want to bump into other vehicles and that I don't want to go through any red lights or exceed the speed limit; it knows just when to rise into the air and accelerate to the appropriate speed, and it knows very well how to take me to my destination without me having to specify it, a detail that my phone or my lighter will have taken care of.

My house knows it has to open up when I arrive at the door, and it knows I need the lights on and a certain temperature to feel comfortable. At the same time it understands that it doesn't have to maintain these conditions when I'm not there and that it can be home or many other things to many other people in many different places.

My house is also home to other people and it is precisely on account of its ability to adapt to anyone that it adapts so well to my needs and makes me feel 'at home'.

It connects not only with me but also with other homes and with other buildings with a range of uses, engaging in dialogue and exchanging data, energy and experience. As do all the other buildings that make up my neighbourhood.

Insofar as I have invested my knowledge and above all my intelligence in the things around me, so they perform accordingly, communicating with one another, raising themselves to the level of my neighbourhood, and from there to the level of my city.

In our vision of the self-sufficient city the city surpasses itself, mimicking all of our positive qualities, making us better, overcoming our limitations and making us more efficient in time.

Our self-sufficient city is dependent. Everything converges in it, and everything is taken from it. In order to subsist, then, it projects itself onto all of the other cities and becomes a planet. It absorbs whatever it can, and always delivers even more. The processes involved in its development are shared, avoiding selfish devices and mechanisms that would corrupt or limit us.

Within the various configurations for self-programming ourselves there is a philosophy that is inert in whatever position. Before opting for a particular setting we must consider our relationship with the universe, our relationship with our species, and find answers to the essential questions. We human beings cannot continue to ignore these questions when we construct our environment, because the way we construct embodies the form in which we believe, and it is first and foremost necessary to be aware of our place on the planet, our place in the universe, in order to transform it accordingly.

At the same time, however, self-sufficiency is achieved not by controlling but by liberating. Up until now we have tried to dominate in order to govern, annihilating the creativity of things, fighting spontaneity as if it were an evil germ, destroying the space for intuition, giving in to our fears. In the self-sufficient city there is no place for fear. There is only a place for commitment, for truth and pain, for engagement with our own nature. So, when it comes to thinking about these configurations that will breathe life into our future development we must commit to ourselves in the deepest sense, the sense that unites us with everything else, that makes us useful to others, that gives us validity beyond ourselves. To be self-sufficient is to have the courage to live up to ourselves, to set ourselves at the level of nature.

Today the options are no longer limitless: the intelligence that was expected of us has been absorbed by artificial forecast systems which spare us endless chores, understand our preferences and anticipate our selections. These systems act beyond our immediate logic, reaching farther and farther, transcending our senses, extending our capabilities, integrating us with all the rest in harmony.

I get into my vehicle which is also the vehicle of others, others get in who are going to the same place as I am, which is also many places and is everyone's.

We are beginning a new unconscious era, the era of settings.

Our city has the job of understanding us, of monitoring the whole complex mesh of interests that leads us to make one decision or another at a particular moment, giving us new places, freeing us from the inconsistency of the habitual, supplying us with the time to rediscover ourselves.

And, above all, it gives us a city our size, a city with room for the quality of things as well as quantity. Leaving the right amount of room for difference, allowing all of the passions to find their place. A city without fear.

HP & IAAC
Santi Morera, Vice-President & General Manager
Large Format Printg Business, Barcelona Site

IaaC is an important partner to HP: As a research and education center, they bring creative ideas, experience and vision of great value to architecture and to HP and we are proud to support them in endeavors like the Self Sufficient City Contest. They participate as a member of HP experts and mentors program among other well renowned architects, designers, photographers and creative professionals from around the world.

Supporting IaaC's initiative and encouraging young architects to work at new concepts of future self sufficient cities and habitat was very meaningful to us. For many years, HP has been seeking to reduce the environmental impact of printing through product development; evidenced by our recent launch of water based Latex Inks which are an alternative to solvent based printing systems. Thus, the idea of this contest was a natural fit between our 2 organizations.

As a market leader in large format architecture and design printing we have worked alongside thousands of architects, engineers and construction experts; providing printing and workflow tools that enabled them to win project bids and draw/edit plans from the beginning of a project to completion. I want to thank all these professionals who have given us feedback and helped to continuously improve our products.

Barcelona hosts HP's worldwide large format printing division and in particular its research and development department. Many of our engineers have been educated by local universities and are now creating printing solutions that simplify the printing workflow to enable architects, engineers, and designers, daily work. It is therefore highly symbolic that we celebrate the 25th anniversary of our Sant Cugat site, the same year as the 150th of the Eixample' Plan, created by an engineer named Ildefons Cerdà. He defined the concept of urbanism which inspired the construction of cities throughout the 19th and 20th centuries, and simultaneously made Barcelona the world flagship in this domain. Barcelona is well known in the world of architecture, represented by such icons as Gaudi and we are happy to be able to continue to support forward thinking organizations like Iaac, which inspire us to think about the world differently. I would like to congratulate the contest winners along with the IaaC organizers and jury for their great choices. Among the 708 participants from 116 countries: the proposals reflected the need to define new paradigms for evolving existing cities, and new rules to generate human habitats that are increasingly compatible with the environmental, economic and social sustainability of our planet. HP wishes you all a great future and career.

ADVANCED ARCHITECTURE CONTEST

This is the third Advanced Architecture Contest to be organized by the IaaC since 2005. The first competition, on the theme of Self-Sufficient Housing, attracted entries from more than 2,500 architects and students from 108 countries, clearly demonstrating the potential of the Internet as a medium for researching new architecture. The special book of the short-listed projects was selected by the RIBA bookshop as one of the best new titles of 2006. The second competition was devoted to The Self-Fab House. The winners of these two previous Advanced Architecture Contests -from France, China and Spain- have completed the IaaC Master course and are currently working in a range of research projects.

ABOUT IAAC

The IaaC is a latest-generation education and research centre with a focus on defining new models of habitat for the 21st century. The IaaC acts as a network within which specialists from a variety of disciplines (ecologists, anthropologists, engineers, computer programmers, artists, sociologists and others) interact with architects in the attaining of knowledge and skills with which to develop advanced architecture. The Institute uses cutting-edge technologies to design and produce prototypes of self-sufficient habitats and works closely with other nodes of knowledge in various cities around the world, as well as participating in the Fab Lab network, effectively furthering our understanding of different realities and acting globally.

ABOUT HP

HP is the world's leading printer brand in architecture and design. its main goal Is exploring and developing technology and services that simplify everyday consumers' and businesses' lives and work. HP cares about its customers' potentials, aspirations and dreams, and it helps to transform them into relevant solutions as well as to grow and evolve side by side with its clients.

HP's imaging and printing group supports iaac's initiatives and projects through the HP experts & mentors program. This program works as a network of architecture, photography, graphic arts and design professionals. Their creative ideas, their experience in printing, and their vision of market trends is of great value to HP.

The Iaac/HP Self Sufficient City contest presents young professionals' creativity and ideas as well as showcasing the great potential of imaging, rendering and architectural design ..

WHY BARCELONA?

The competition coincides with the 150th anniversary of the Eixample Plan for Barcelona, drawn up by the engineer Ildefons Cerdà, which did so much to define the concept of urbanism that served to guide construction of cities throughout the 19th and 20th centuries.

From this starting point, participants reflected on the need to define new paradigms for the recycling of existing cities, and the need for new rules with which to build in continuity with nature, in such a way as to generate spaces for human habitability that contribute to the environmental, economic and social sustainability of the planet.

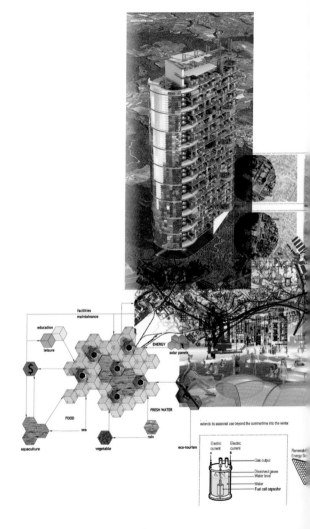

facilities
maintainance

education

leisure

ENERGY

solar panels

$

FRESH WATER

FOOD

sea

rain

aquaculture

vegetable

eco-tourism

extends its seasonal use beyond the summertime into the winter

Electric current A | Electric current B
Gas output
Dissolved gases
Water level
Water
Fuel cell capacitor

Renewable
Energy S

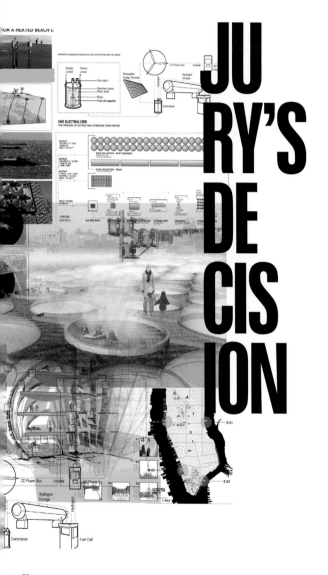

JU
RY'S
DE
CIS
ION

JURY

Cooperating via internet during October and November 708 proposals from 116 countries were evaluated by the following jury members of the 3rd Advanced Architecture Contest

Jaime Lerner — Architect, former Mayor of Curitiba, former President of UIA
Mr. Mityrev — Representative for the Governor of Saint Petersburg
Brett Steele — Director of the Architectural Association, London
Stan T. Allen — Dean of Princeton University School of Architecture
Yung Ho Chang — Head of the MIT Department of Architecture
Aaron Betsky — Director of The Cincinnati Art Museum
Haakon Karlsen Jr — Director of MIT Fab Lab Norway
Pankaj Joshi — Director of Urbanism Design Research Institute. Mumbai, India
Benyam Ali — Head of the Addis Ababa University Department of Architecture
J.M. Lin — Architect, The Observer Design Group, Taiepi, Taiwan
Bostian Vuga — Sadar & Vuga architects, Lubjana , Slovenia
Michel Rojkind — Rojkind Arquitecto, México
Vicente Guallart — Director of IAAC, Barcelona
Willy Müller — Director of IAAC Development
Marta Male-Alemany — Co-director of IAAC Master in Advanced Architecture
Areti Markopoulou — Academic Coordinator of IAAC Master in Advanced Architecture
Lucas Cappelli — Director of 3rd Advanced Architecture Contest

Each juror has selected a first, second, and third prize, and honourable mentions in some cases. The jury voted on 28 proposals which have demonstrated great diversity and vision of the habitat of the future.

The jury has decided to award the following contestants:

HURBS

Sergio Castillo Tello, María Hernández Enríquez

Spain

Hybrid Human Urban Re-adaptive Bidirectionally-Relational System that proposed the creation of a participatory experiment in order to develop an urban informational system in which the citizens and experts work together to develop cities through solutions that optimize urban resources. The jury acknowledges this vision of a city as a structure that is re-informed through digital management systems.

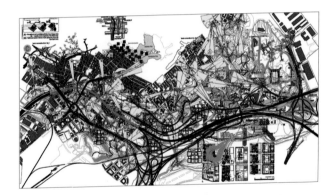

WATER FUEL

Rychiee Espinosa, Seth McDowell

United States

Proposed the development of technologies that transform salt water into energy, generating hydrogen in urban environments, to be utilized for transportation systems and urban consumption. The jury acknowledges this as the integration of energy production systems into an urban context and it's ability to transform civic environments and foment the generation of energy by means of self-sufficiency. These structures have been well designed and are capable of urban landscape integration.

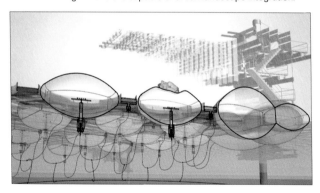

The jury has agreed to give 4 honourable mentions to the following proposals:

SKY CITY

Designed by Victor Kirillow from Russia who proposed the construction of urban mega structures, in which the city is stacked vertically to protect it's green spaces, giving access to each level through future transportation systems..

MOBILIZING VILLAGES

Designed by Do Trung Kien from Vietnam, who proposed a floating city off the coast of Vietnam, with forms that abstract the surrounding landscapes, approaching the question "Is it possible to rise above sea level?", and its effect on coastal cities.

RECIPROCITY

Designed by Jason Butz, Frank D'Andrea, Carla Landa, Martha Skinner from the United States who proposed the creation of recycling structures which recycle urban waste and capable of creating materials of high architectural design for urban reuse.

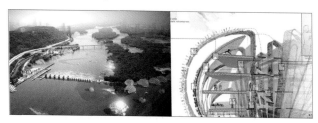

MASSIVE URBAN RECYCLING

designed by Adrian Garcia, Douglas Rodriguez from Mexico who proposed to recycle urban obsolete structures, incorporating new functions such as domestic functions, without destroying prominent urban buildings, when they've lost their function.

The jury would like to thank the effort carried out by all contestants, and encourages the development of ideas which transform cities into more stimulating environments for the human life.

PARTICIPANTS

2492 registered participants
708 proposals
116 countries participating

United States[217]
Mexico[216]
Spain[163]
France[118]
Russian[113]
Chile[103]
India[103]
Italy[99]
United Kingdom[94]
Colombia[71]
Serbia Montenegro[63]
Argentina[58]
Brazil[52]
Korea Republic[51]
Afghanistan[50]
Israel[37]
Venezuela[37]
Australia[37]
China[36]
Germany[36]
Portugal[36]
Romania[34]
Canada[32]
Greece[29]
Indonesia[27]
Ukraine[27]
Egypt[26]
Netherlands[24]
Peru[21]
Ireland[20]
Iran[19]
Poland[18]
Uruguay[17]
Ecuador[16]

Hungary[16]
Vietnam[16]
Turkey[16]
Costa Rica[15]
Belgium[15]
Bulgaria[14]
Taiwan[14]
Philippines[12]
Malaysia[11]
Japan[11]
Singapore[11]
Hong Kong[10]
Austria[9]
Algeria[9]
Georgia[8]
Croatia[8]
Bolivia[8]
Dominican Republic[8]
Thailand[7]
Macedonia[7]
Syrian[6]
Bosnia/Herzegovina[6]
Pakistan[6]
Nigeria[5]
South Africa[5]
Lithuania[5]

Latvia[5]
El Salvador[5]
Guatemala[5]
Denmark[4]
Belarus[4]
Kazakstan[4]
Saudi Arabia[4]
New Zealand[4]
Jordan[4]
Sri[4]
Tunisia[4]
Iceland[3]
Puerto Rico[3]
Czech Republic[3]

Nepal[3]
Switzerland[3]
Lebanon[3]
Bangladesh[3]
Albania[3]
Armenia[3]
Korea Democratic[3]
Zimbabwe[3]
Montenegro[2]
Arab Emirates[2]
Uganda[2]
Morocco[2]
Iraq[2]
Cuba[2]

Azerbaijan[2]
Finland[2]
Sweden[2]
Moldova[2]
Estonia[2]
Slovakia[2]
Ethiopia[2]
Equatorial Guinea[2]
Libyan[2]
Kenya[2]
Malta[2]
Jamaica[2]
Angola[2]
Norway[2]

Saint Helena[1]
American Samoa[1]
Yemen[1]
Myanmar[1]
Cayman Islands[1]
Togo[1]
Eritrea[1]
Saint Lucia[1]
Honduras[1]
Panama[1]
Nicaragua[1]
Zambia[1]
Cyprus[1]
Palestinian[1]

FINALISTS PROJECTS

708 participants from 116 countries,
107 finalists from 34 countries

- 21st century city - an urban future
- A model for the return to sustainable city life?
- A vision for trivandrum 2035 ad
- Abstract city: Ukraine
- Amdixon – new boston
- Architecture as infrastructure
- Bauci 2040
- Bio digital city
- Canary wharf + poplar - London 2015
- Capsule housing
- City a & h
- City and country - BSAS 2050
- City factory
- Cloud garden
- Constanta city
- Continu city
- Continuous city
- Cyarch - Cybernetic extraterrestral architecture
- De-pave Chicago
- Desertification barrier
- Dispersed town - urbanized village or rural town
- Dissolved
- Do androids dream of electronic garden
- Dokdo
- Drift city a continental transient infra structure
- Eco sin compensator
- Eco.Necting
- Ecologic urban model – an idea of a city
- Ecotopia
- Environmental_hub
- Evolving urbanity
- Extension self-sufficientnetworkingap paratus
- Farm city
- Filter tower - the self sufficient building
- Fitting systems
- Fomc fields of metabolic cleansers
- Freedom in captivity
- Green city
- Green transplant: an ecological blast wave on the city.
- Greening the city, connecting communities
- Growing a prototypical urban alga-farmland
- H20 hels.Hyv.Oulu - Helsinki 2060
- H2090
- Hurbs
- Holecity
- Humanity's answer to nature's quest... Edifice 2045
- Hydroponic farmers market
- Lifeline
- Living system
- Madrid 20xx
- Massive urban recycling
- Mega city block
- Melbourne 2030
- Membrane city - no centre, no limits, smart evolution

- Meteorite / beijing 2080
- Mobilizing village
- Natural talent
- New urban economies
- Nombre del proyecto
- Non stop city
- One cubic kilometer city
- Orchard tower
- Organic futuristic phenomenon floating cityball
- Photosynthesis hex-a-gone
- Poetic recorded vestige
- Raining building
- Reciprocity
- Repower city
- Right to be itself (sufficient)
- Rurban settlement
- Santa monica algae farm (bio-architecture)
- Sea farm city – problem statement
- Self-equipped be a pleasing place to ing
- Self-sufficient city copenhagen
- Sidery
- Sky city
- Slopscraper: dirty tech for the clean city of tomorrow
- Soak city
- Socioecological-trees
- Space and lies
- Strand city
- Submergia
- Super mangrovescape, pro-resort urbanism
- Swarm city
- Symbiotic entities
- Symbiotic landscape
- Synergetic system
- Techno-ecologies
- The agrarian field + field landscape
- The city power of 10
- The conceptual decision of the self-regulating building
- The fluid network
- The inverted city: dubai 2050
- The nomad city the city like you
- The self sufficient building / shapes of the mountains
- The self sustaining city system
- The waffle house@bamboo lake
- The weightlessness city
- Third belgrade
- Urban agriculture
- Urban corridor
- Water and the city Copenhagen + Helsinki
- Water fuel a water-fueled scooter network
- Water fuel the plan for a self-sustaining New York City
- Waterwheel
- What happens when city arrives to nature?
- Zmvm

vertical engineering &
transport & pedestrian
service lines

wind generator

solar battery
HAIR DU TEMPS

LE PURE CAFE

ground level

public services & transportation
community shopping centre

transport level

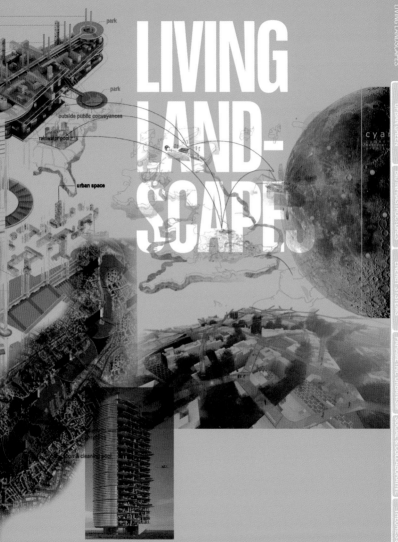

park

park

outside public conveyances

rainwater pool

urban space

main & cleaning pool

LIVING LAND- SCAPES

cya

LIVING LANDSCAPES

URBAN GREEN

BIO INFRASTRUCTURES

ENERGY SYSTEMS

PARAMETRIC URBANISM

SOCIAL & COLLABORATIVE

THEORIES & STRATEGIES

LIVING LANDSCAPES

The origins of the word landscape have to do with the shape of a terrain, with the way nature or eventually culture acts on and affects the land. 'Living Landscapes' takes a close-up look at the way new self-sufficient projects shape the silhouette of cities.

Is it possible to think Architecture on the basis of time more than space? Trans-formation is the core of modern culture, time lapses embrace change and rapid, fast and speedy have become today's premises. Time rules, and to experience it, to experience duration is to experience plasticity, dilation, flux, movement. The city changes its shapes and forms according to the needs of its inhabitants.

In this context, projects are liable to manifest a tendency towards de-materializing; the use of intelligent and programmable materials tends not to separate but to join, to multiply, to let energy flow. Quick and easy modifications, speedy disassemblies and flexible dynamic structures multiply the chances of encapsulating a self-sufficient process. These projects try to explore a concept of city that is not just the sum of buildings and roads but a living organism growing towards an uncertain future. To make this future more manageable, certain core elements of landscape and its uses must be submitted to a reconsideration: water supply, waste processing, transportation networks and the location of productive units and leisure areas. The options include urban growth along vertical axes; ecological computing systems to monitor and manage energy and water; multiple interlinked ecosystems metabolizing resources and waste; ultra-mobile, flexible 'g-force free' buildings; water systems that redefine the landscape entirely; the void of the street replaced by solid linear buildings; cities with no axes, monuments or lines; moving dwellings, and agro-ecosystems within the city.

Self-sufficient design can help us re-use, recycle and even beautify the bad and remind us of endemic growth, minimizing the effects of the cycles of decline in the modern city.

A flexible, 'living' landscape is the necessary result of embracing this tendency and adjusting it to the existing boundaries of space.

LIVING LANDSCAPES

URBAN GREEN

BIO INFRASTRUCTURES

ENERGY SYSTEMS

PARAMETRIC URBANISM

SOCIAL & COLLABORATIVE

THEORIES & STRATEGIES

SECOND NATURE IN THE THIRD CITY DEPAVE CHICAGO

Justin Petersen

jpeterse@umich.edu

United States

In the 19th Century Chicago grew faster than city any in the world by eagerly exploiting the North American landscape, redistributing its resources, slaughtering its livestock and reversing its rivers. It was, by many accounts, the most horrifically polluted and violent urban machine that man had ever created. In the 20th Century Chicago exemplified the rise, fall and rebirth of the American Metropolis. A city of radical contrasts and big shoulders, Chicago does not borrow its sublime power from a surrounding landscape, it constructs it by design. This city, in other words, is the unabashed product of modern civilization, one of the most thoroughly architectural cities in the World. It is the epitome of the best and worst that we have to offer each other. This project proposes a series of strategic modifications to Chicago's existing infrastructure in order to cultivate a self-sufficient pattern of development over the course of the next century. These interventions primarily encourage the development of high-density nodes surrounded by more typical urban neighborhoods and agricultural spaces. More than an exercise in efficiency, these proposals re-imagine the city as a hybrid environment of intense, layered relationships that challenge cultural perceptions of urbanity, domesticity and wilderness.

De-Paving the City

A prioritization of the automobile as the principle means of transportation remains the primary barrier to creating a more sustainable pattern of living in America. This project thus confronts the automobile and specifically de-prioritizes it through a progressive de-paving of the city over the course of the next fifty years. The project does not intend to dramatically remove or alter the street pattern of Chicago, which is understood to be vital to the urban environment. Instead, designated side streets are to be replaced by narrow porous lanes, thus retaining access for service vehicles and small electric cars or bicycles.

LIVING LANDSCAPES

URBAN GREEN

BIO INFRASTRUCTURES

ENERGY SYSTEMS

PARAMETRIC URBANISM

SOCIAL & COLLABORATIVE

THEORIES & STRATEGIES

LIVING LANDSCAPES

URBAN GREEN

BIO-INFRASTRUCTURES

ENERGY SYSTEMS

PARAMETRIC URBANISM

SOCIAL & COLLABORATIVE

THEORIES & STRATEGIES

THE INVERTED CITY: DUBAI 2050

Ming Tan

mtangmsu@hotmail.com

China

The central feature of this project is the design a new city infrastructure network for ensuring it will provide a self-sufficient urban development by inverting the current urban fabric. On top of the current urban infrastructure, which is usually following the street network, several new components such as vertical farm (with irrigation and bio-mass and recycle system), miles long linear residential and mixed use space on top of the street, green space filling the city blocks are integrated as a new comprehensive infrastructure. By adding a series large scale vertical farm and inverting the void street network into solid linear building volumes, this project reveals and reclaims the characteristics of city's original figure ground, and make the original building sites available again for future urban agriculture and recreational development.

LIVING LANDSCAPES

URBAN GREEN

BIO INFRASTRUCTURES

ENERGY SYSTEMS

PARAMETRIC URBANISM

SOCIAL & COLLABORATIVE

THEORIES & STRATEGIES

LIVING LANDSCAPES

URBAN GREEN

BIO INFRASTRUCTURES

ENERGY SYSTEMS

PARAMETRIC URBANISM

SOCIAL & COLLABORATIVE

THEORIES & STRATEGIES

THE WEIGHTLESSNESS CITY

Olivier Terrisse

oliv_terrisse@hotmail.com

France

The weightlessness city is an utopian reality. It's caring and poetic. It may be a near or distant future. It forgets Newton's discovery to redefine the concept of the city. It tackle issues like functionnal mixed, urban sprawl or urban congestion to create the self sufficient city of the future.

Concept 01
The conservation, collective memory, the existing
The self sufficient city already exists , the majority of buildings from the late 21st century has already been built. We don't have to destroy, we have to maintain, improve and complete through the weightlessness city.

Concept 02
Most mobility
Travel has to be released. They shouldn't be restrained in a plan by a concentric or radiating network. The networks previously generating cuts, dead spaces, urban pockets, blocking, functional zoning, becomes obsolete. Moving will be again RES PUBLICA.

Concept 03
Most compact
Urban sprawl is synonymous of waste, of time, of money, raw material, spaces, ecosystem and earth. The planar city has lived. The city has to be now in three dimensions, in weightlessnes.

Concept 04
Most flexible
Buildings, previously rooted to the ground, is going to be free of the gravitational force. It can move freely to meet their needs. The function will again become functional. The dwelling will always be close to work, work will always be close to home. The necessary industry for these new uses already exists, it's the recycling of the auto industry at the end of cycle.

An open planar city : thanks to the general densification offered by the weightless world but can also give back a mobility, then can permit to restore. It serves the parisian choice who no longer meet the standards of comfort and can't be refurbish will be cleared out and replaced by parks.

LIVING LANDSCAPES

URBAN GREEN

BIO INFRASTRUCTURES

ENERGY SYSTEMS

PARAMETRIC URBANISM

SOCIAL & COLLABORATIVE

THEORIES & STRATEGIES

Concept 05 : Most mixed

The new proximity created by the couple's home-work will create a continuous functional carpet self-regulated, perfect, free of any law, any incitement

An extreme density on an existing area : the weightlessness city occupies the sky as an hemisphere. This is the most efficient natural volume.

The city is no longer fixed : it is moving. Urban time is compressed to everyday

life. Possibilities are endless. The choice of location is anymore synonymous of rooting, the nanos centralities born, evolve, grow and sometimes die according to new affinity.

A parisian nano centrality : housing, shops, a small factory, a café, a hairdresser, an exhibition gallery, a post office ... The nano centrality is in perpetual metamorphosis due to the live of its inhabitants .

Weightlessness : the easiness of movings will change the everyday life. There will

The city is no longer fixed : it is moving. Urban time is compressed to everyday life. Possibilities are endless. The choice of location is anymore synonymous of rooting, the nanos centralities born, evolve, grow and sometimes die according to new affinity.

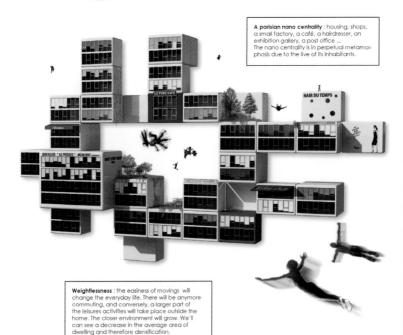

A parisian nano centrality : housing, shops, a small factory, a café, a hairdresser, an exhibition gallery, a post office ...
The nano centrality is in perpetual metamorphosis due to the live of its inhabitants.

Weightlessness : the easiness of movings will change the everyday life. There will be anymore commuting, and conversely, a larger part of the leisures activities will take place outside the home. The closer environment will grow. We'll can see a decrease in the average area of dwelling and therefore densification.

LIVING LANDSCAPES

URBAN GREEN

BIO INFRASTRUCTURES

ENERGY SYSTEMS

PARAMETRIC URBANISM

SOCIAL & COLLABORATIVE

THEORIES & STRATEGIES

be anymore commuting, and conversely, a larger part of the leisures activities will take place outside of the home. The closer environment will grow. We'll can see a decrease in the average area of dwelling and therefore densification.

The weightlessness city of Paris : the weightlessness city is not an international fact, it has the same environmental quality than the planar city. In the sky of Paris, we will find the same atmosphere and the same charm than the historic Paris. These unique features are related to French and Parisian culture.

An open planar city : beyond the general densification offered by the weightlessness city, it can also give back a portion of urban ground to nature. Therefore the parisian blocks who no longer meet the standarts of comfort and can't be refurbish will be destroyed and replaced by park.

A sustainable colonization : we will be more than 9 billion earthlings in 2050. Although densification is one way, the conquest of new territories is essential. The weightlessness city is the best way to preserve the natural ground and our planet.

Full mixed : the physical and administrative boundaries of the city are often the cause of functional or social zooning . The weightlessness city is free from this forced separation.

New flexibility : the possibility of moving for any reason and especially for any length, become infinite.

New Mobility: at an town scale or a district scale, the movement is released, densified, optimized, thinned…

SKY CITY

Kirillow Victor

kir.architect@inbox.ru

Russia

The project "Sky City" is an attempt to understand the positive and negative tendencies of modern urban planning. The modern system of urban planning formed under the influence of many factors such as: historical, technical, economic, social, etc. The underlying factor of the system is its self-regulation, each element (building) appears only when it is necessary to society and it is determined above listed factors. Today, we are improving the urban planning unit (building) and little attention on the struc-ture which has a long time is unchanged. Also present and negative factors such as: urban sprawl, the eternal conflict of pedestrian and traffic flow, proximity to industrial zones, high density areas, poor insolation, etc.

"Sky City" is a rethinking of modern urban structure while preserving its positive trends. Vertical development environment protects the biosphere. Platform is a space to fill urban development units and are a factor of flexibility as well as retain the notion of street - the building, the alternation of open and closed spaces. Multi-level platforms share the flows of pedestrians and transport, and operate in continuous mode. Also the city is endowed with a closed engineering and power system.

This project does not search for new forms and new space is merely an attempt to look at the urban structure from a different angle and attempt to solve real problems. Aesthetics of the structure in its rationality, functionality, viability, and I believe that they are the key to self-sufficiency !

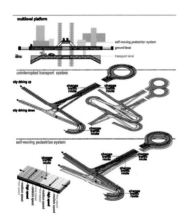

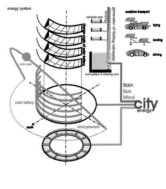

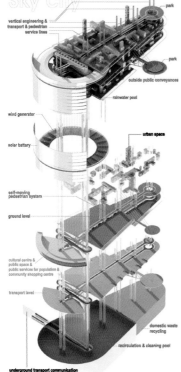

functional scheme
sky city

park

vertical engineering &
transport & pedestrian
service lines

park

outside public conveyances

rainwater pool

wind generator

solar battery

urban space

self-moving
pedestrian system

ground level

cultural centre &
public space &
public services for population &
community shopping centre

transport level

domestic waste
recycling

recirculation & cleaning pool

underground transport communication

LIVING LANDSCAPES

URBAN GREEN

BIO-INFRASTRUCTURES

ENERGY SYSTEMS

PARAMETRIC URBANISM

SOCIAL & COLLABORATIVE

THEORIES & STRATEGIES

LIVING LANDSCAPES

URBAN GREEN

BIO INFRASTRUCTURES

ENERGY SYSTEMS

PARAMETRIC URBANISM

SOCIAL & COLLABORATIVE

THEORIES & STRATEGIES

BIO-DIGITAL CITY

Bailly Claire
J. Magerand
L. Bruneau
J. Jullien
E.-S. Bae
N. Purseramen
M. Reina

claire@bailly.as

France

Location: plateau de Saclay, Ile-de-France, France; in the National Interest Operation of Versailles-Saclay-Massy-St Quentin

> 30 000 housings are to be built in this area. The city is conceived as an artificial eco-system, a para-living organism.

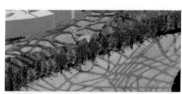

Urban agriculture

Agro-ecosystem lines curve are set between the construction lines, generating continuous biological spaces. Some of these spaces are reserved for biodiversity, others to walk, or to purify the water, or are collective or individual gardens. The major part is devoted to a profitable agriculture and horticulture.

Ecological Computing

Micro-biological sensors, chemical caloriphiques, physical, volumetric, phonic pressuremeter, etc. are densely distributed throughout the city to analyze all the symptoms related to Urban biological environment, in real time.

Energy

Energy is produced continuously (gravity water, solar, wind, thermal sensors, brake transport, domestic methane generators) and is stored. It is reintroduced into the grid as far as it is needed.

Multirecycling

A part of recycling takes place in the buildings basements.

What can not be treated at the scale of a single building is treated across the neighborhood. The equipemtns are shared. The surplus is valued in peri-urban agricultural purposes.

Green machines

Robots collect, identify, and sort all the wastes. They maintain all networks. They gather plants in the basements lagoons, grind them, compost them, carry them to the growing areas in need.

LIVING LANDSCAPES

URBAN GREEN

BIO-INFRASTRUCTURES

ENERGY SYSTEMS

PARAMETRIC URBANISM

SOCIAL & COLLABORATIVE

THEORIES & STRATEGIES

LIVING LANDSCAPES

URBAN GREEN

BIO INFRASTRUCTURES

ENERGY SYSTEMS

PARAMETRIC URBANISM

SOCIAL & COLLABORATIVE

THEORIES & STRATEGIES

TECHNO-ECOLOGIES

Bas Bobrova Daniel
Javier Alonso Ojembarrena

danibas.bob@gmail.com

Spain

Emergence. Any aim to promote self-sufficiency proposal must encourage emerging states. We take those emerging states also as models for action on recently-built and unsustainable urban environments.

Tecnological-ecosystems. Human environment consists of a technological set of organisms. They are able to form self-sufficient systems increasing the number of relationships. Architecture doesn't exist if it is not installed on its environmental natural cycles.

Technological-niche. We have related in nature, its organizational ecosystem models, climate control systems and energy production. Relationship between organisms is based in mutualism, commensalism, parasitism and competition.

Data-management. Urban environment has to do with resource management. To generate a model, complex systems are required. Organisms perform as self-balanced communities due to the data-network established between them.

Boundary-conditions. To prevent a project in a situationist approach, its environmental issues are its own boundary conditions. Their installation-colonization of urban space generates an altered and free urban action through the accumulation of elements.

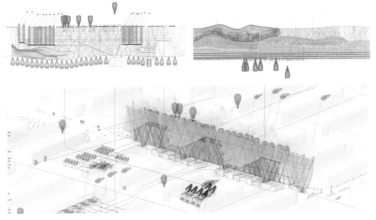

> *Techno-ecologies*

–

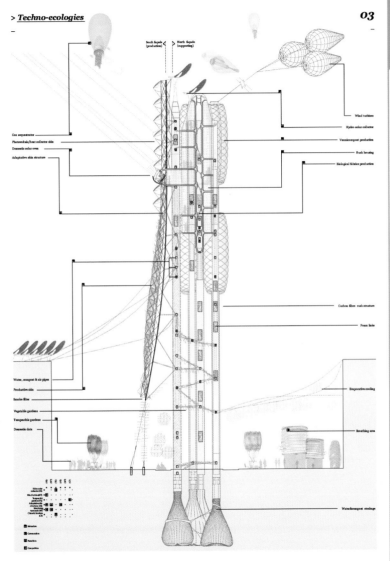

South façade (production) North façade (supporting)

Gas sequestrator
Photovoltaic/heat collector skin
Domestic solar oven
Adaptative skin structure

Wind turbines
Hydro-solar collector
Vermicompost production
Rush housing
Biological fabrics production

Carbon fibre rush structure

Foam linin

Water, seatpost & air pipes
Productive skin
Smoke filter
Vegetable gardens
Therapeutic gardens
Domestic data

Evaporative cooling

Breathing area

Water&compost stockage

03

LIVING LANDSCAPES

URBAN GREEN

BIO-INFRASTRUCTURES

ENERGY SYSTEMS

PARAMETRIC URBANISM

SOCIAL & COLLABORATIVE

THEORIES & STRATEGIES

DISSOLVED

Garcia Pedron
Alejandro
Raquel Sola Rubio

cruxflux.net@gmail.com

Spain

Social organizations are changing. People are not interested in politics anymore , we don't feel part of our city. But on the other hand, we are developing a new identity. This (new identity) and part of our personal relationships are complex nodes in the network, our amplified nature. We define ourselves through connections. Dissolved and flat hierarchies. Free associations, "the noble savage" has returned. We propose a land management and urban administration according to this current social features. Completely egalitarian, where each man or woman is responsible of his space and can discard, customize, sell or move it. The city will grow without lines, axis or monuments.. The current house is a prison for our new experiences and a tomb for environmental resources. We will dissolve the house into the city and the infrastructure. Nomadism. The needs being satisfied on the outside. A dismembered house, changing and shared. We are transparent, and we want to be seen.

We consider the change as progress. Today's city will be like one more layer of the earth. Let's collect its fruits, energy, and give back the green that we asphalted.

We will grow from this root as a crystalline leaf, that flee from the forms and just looks for its dissolution.

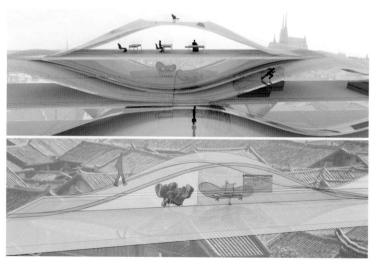

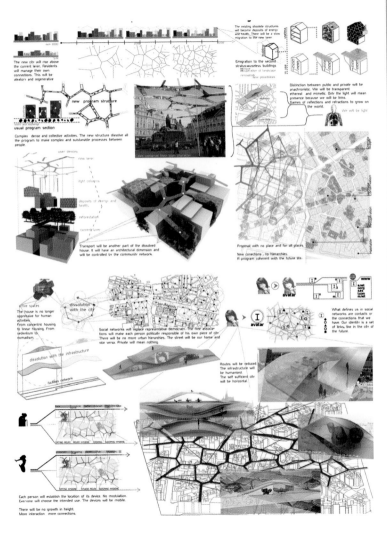

LIVING LANDSCAPES

URBAN GREEN

BIG INFRASTRUCTURES

ENERGY SYSTEMS

PARAMETRIC URBANISM

SOCIAL & COLLABORATIVE

THEORIES & STRATEGIES

The new city will rise above the current layer. Residents will manage their own connections. This will be aleatory and regenerative.

The existing obsolete structures will become deposits of energy and health. There will be a slow migration to the new layer.

Emigration to the second stratum useless buildings

Distinction between public and private will be anachronistic. We will be transparent ethereal and mimetic. Only the light will mean presence because we will be links. Games of reflections and refractions to grow on the world.

We will be light

new program structure

usual program section

Complex dense and collective activities. The new structure dissolve all the program to make complex and sustainable processes between people.

user devices

new layer

light columns

deposits of energy and health.

reforestation

current layer

Transport will be another part of the dissolved house. It will have an architectural dimension and will be controlled by the community network.

Proposal with no place and for all places.

New connections . no hierarchies.
A program coherent with the future life.

active spaces

The house is no longer oppressive for human activities. From concentric housing to linear housing. From sedentism to nomadism.

dissolution with the city

dissolution with the infrastructure

facilities network

Social networks will replace representative democracy. The free associations will make each person politically responsible of his own piece of city. There will be no more urban hierarchies. The street will be our home and vice versa. Private will mean nothing.

avatar

What defines us in social networks are contacts or the connections that we have. Our identity is a set of links, like in the city of the future.

Routes will be reduced. The infrastructure will be humanized. The self sufficient city will be horizontal.

Each person will establish the location of its device. No modulation. Everyone will choose the intended use. The devices will be mobile.

There will be no growth in height. More interaction . more connections.

LIVING LANDSCAPES

URBAN GREEN

BIO-INFRASTRUCTURES

ENERGY SYSTEMS

PARAMETRIC URBANISM

SOCIAL & COLLABORATIVE

THEORIES & STRATEGIES

MEMBRANE CITY - NO CENTRE, NO LIMITS, SMART EVOLUTION

Alexandrova Elena

alena.alexandrova@yahoo.com

RUSSIAN FEDERATION

Membrane City is an organism with a cellular texture. It involves cells of different form and size according to their functions, but all cells have a similar structure. Every cell consists of a main body, a buffer zone and a membrane.

A main body forms a cell. It presents a function that cannot be mixed with dwelling and infrastructure and demand large areas.

All these functions need a buffer zone between the main body and the membrane. It has influence on a size and a form of each cell.

A membrane is a complex of functions that can be mixed and work together more efficiently than in separation. It circles every cell and has two levels. On the 1st level there are production, offices and car roads. The 2nd level represents dwelling, infrastructure and recreation. The park on 1st level buildings roofs is for pedestrian and bicycle traffic and recreation.

View from the 1st level of the membrane.

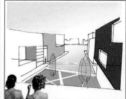
View from the roof park of the membrane .

The inner yard of production building in the membrane.

View from the centre of the cell to the membrane.

View from the 2nd level of the membrane.

Membrane City - no centre, no limits, smart evolution.

View to the dwelling group with cooling pond of production building.

LIVING LANDSCAPES

URBAN GREEN

BIO-INFRASTRUCTURES

ENERGY SYSTEMS

PARAMETRIC URBANISM

SOCIAL & COLLABORATIVE

THEORIES & STRATEGIES

Agriculture

Agriculture system involves large scale plots (farmlands) as the main function of the cell and small scale private farming plots in membrane of each cell.
This reduces the distance food has to travel from field to fork.

Recycling

Item for sustaining Eco-Cycle and creating the invironment with Zero Waste.

Green zone

Nature conservancy zon animal migration paths and exsisting natural systems are taken into account.

Energy

Renewable energy sources (wind trbines, solar panels, or bio-gas created from sewage).
In addition to energy production in large scale, there are local energy systems in membrane of each cell.

Production

There are production of different scale. Large areas in the main body are for factories and plants. Production with appropriate technology and business zones are mixed with other functions in the membrane. As a result, people live closer to the workspace and dormitory suburbs are not forming.

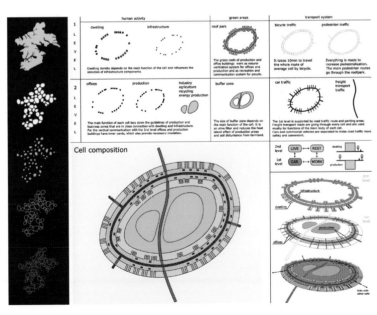

	human activity		green areas	transport system	
1 LEVEL	dwelling	infrastructure	roof park	bicycle traffic	pedestrian traffic
	Dwelling density depends on the main function of the cell and influences the selection of infrastructure components.		The green roofs of production and office buildings work as natural ventilation system for offices and production and as recreation and communication system for people.	It takes 10min to travel the whole route of average cell by bicycle.	Everything is made to increase pedestrialization. The main pedestrian routes go through the roofpark.
2 LEVEL	offices	production agriculture recycling energy production	buffer zone	car traffic	freight transport traffic
	The main function of each cell lays down the guidelines of production and business zones that are in close connection with dwelling and infrastructure. For the vertical communication with the 2nd level offices and production buildings have inner yards, which also provide necessary insolation.		The size of buffer zone depends on the main function of the cell. It is an alive filter and reduces the heat island effect of production areas and soil disturbance from farmland.	The 1st level is supported by road traffic route and parking areas. Freight transport roads are going through every cell and are used mostly for functions of the main body of each cell. Cars and commercial vehicles are separated to make road traffic more safety and convenient.	

Cell composition

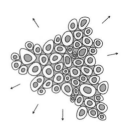

Excisting Village

Arable land of the village

Частая Дубрава · Частая Дубрава

Excisting Village

Excisting village

Excisting village

52°27'00.57" C   39°27'40.86" B

LIVING LANDSCAPES

URBAN GREEN

BIO-INFRASTRUCTURES

ENERGY SYSTEMS

PARAMETRIC URBANISM

SOCIAL & COLLABORATIVE

THEORIES & STRATEGIES

CYARCH - CYBERNETIC EXTRATERRESTRAL ARCHITECTURE

L David
d0_up
dlm85.sbd@gmail.com

Spain

WHAT WOULD HAPPEN IF WE HAD TO LEAVE THE EARTH?

Whether our home gets damaged or the environment gets radically transformed, we immediately think about the necessity to change, of course, always with the idea of improvement. Taking into account this atmosphere we might imagine the extraordinary possibilities The Moon offers, for instance, to create a conceptually new architecture. The city improved organized in extraterrestrial environment with a magnificent emptyness, a lunar community permanent and self-sufficient. Slender structures taking advantage of the low gravitational force.
Connection channels for immediate movements.

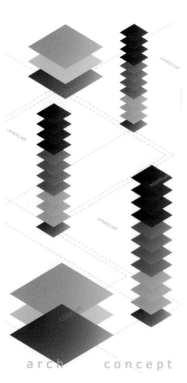

arch   concept

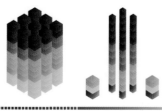

CURRENT MODEL CITY   NEW MODEL CITY

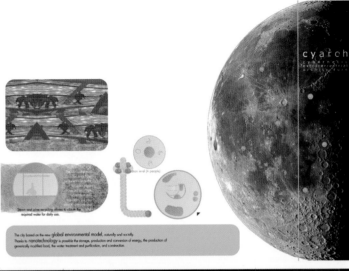

cyarch
cybernetic
extraterrestrial
architecture

Steam and urine recycling allows to obtain the required water for daily use.

The city based on the new global environmental model, naturally and socially.
Thanks to nanotechnology is possible the storage, production and conversion of energy, the production of genetically modified food, the water treatment and purification, and construction.

LIVING LANDSCAPES

URBAN GREEN

BIO INFRASTRUCTURES

ENERGY SYSTEMS

PARAMETRIC URBANISM

SOCIAL & COLLABORATIVE

THEORIES & STRATEGIES

THE SELF SUSTAINING CITY SYSTEM

Elston Emma
Isobel Ward

emma.f.elston@googlemail.com

United Kingdom

Future London is a collection of independent and interlinked ecosystems that metabolise their resources and waste to supply inhabitants, and which operate through symbiotic exchange with other self sustaining city ecosystems. Trade in skills and resources creates self perpetuating and self regulating relationships at global and city scales and allows the city to adapt to future scenarios such as rising water levels through a series of complex bio-mimicry processes The floodzone of the Thames has created opportunities for greater biodiversity by replenishing nutrients in the soil and forcing the city to embrace rooftop farming, allowing all inhabitants to come into contact with the natural ecosystem which sustains them. By simulating nature, creating a complex and diverse habitat for all living forms, and through the cultivation of hybrid bio-technologies, all the city's resources are self supplied, and waste is used to provide energy for the city's processes. Insectoid energy suppliers allow excess energy to be put back into an international energy grid, while micro bio regulators regulate the environment through the absorption of harmful substances and the fractional regulation of temperatures. The city requires nurture and care by all who inhabit it, but in return it provides food energy and shelter; this relationship is appreciated and essential.

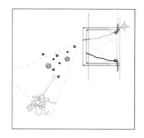

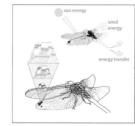

scale : micro

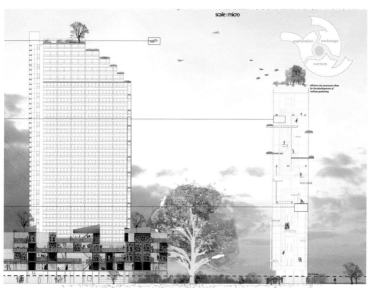

LIVING LANDSCAPES

URBAN GREEN

BIO INFRASTRUCTURES

ENERGY SYSTEMS

PARAMETRIC URBANISM

SOCIAL & COLLABORATIVE

THEORIES & STRATEGIES

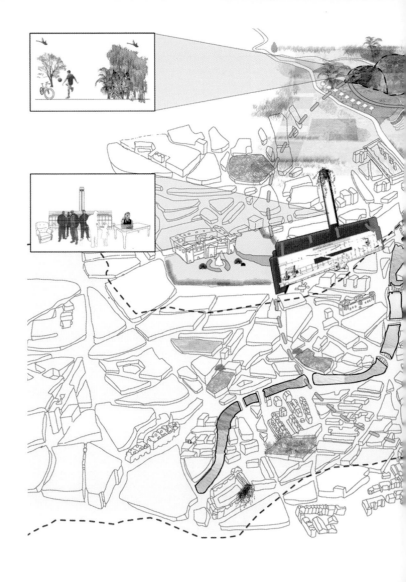

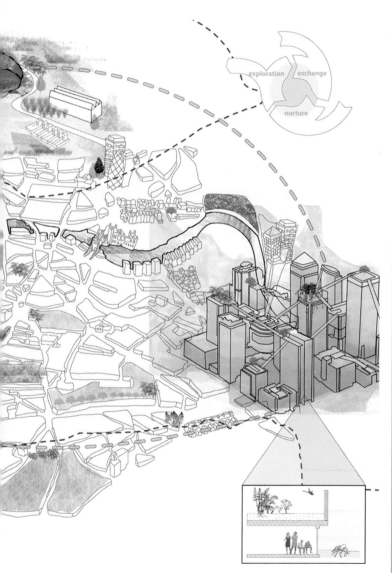

exploration — exchange — nurture

LIVING LANDSCAPES

URBAN GREEN

BIO INFRASTRUCTURES

ENERGY SYSTEMS

PARAMETRIC URBANISM

SOCIAL & COLLABORATIVE

THEORIES & STRATEGIES

THE FLUID NETWORK

Zhihang Luo
Rose Ling-Yee Hung
Ying Liu
Meng Yang
hylesor@gmail.com

United Kingdom

A self-sufficient network which utilizes, emerges with and recycle the natural resources determined the future growth and prosperity of the city. The design explored new water management and utilization strategies to approach the design of a new self-sufficient urban network. The project envisioned the future water-infrastructure as a self-sustainable and ecological network that accommodates our transportation, ecology, energy and recreational systems in cities.

In the project, traditional road network is replaced by the shallow-draft water transportation, which spent 1.5 times less energy than rail and 5 times less than vehicles. Energy zone for the harvest of hydroelectricity and natural zone as a natural preserve. Recreational and ecology programs enhance the better water treatment and human connection with water, such as wetland, natural preserve and inland waterways/ parks. The interconnected architectural envelope also performed as a continuous skin of solar, wind energy generator, water treatment plant as well as rain-water connection storage.

1 EXISTING SITE

2 SELF SUFFICIENT WATER NETWORK

3 COMMERICAL AND OPEN SPACE SYSTEMS

4 HUMAN GROWTH, SETTLEMENT PATTERN

5 CITY FORMED

6 CITY GROW

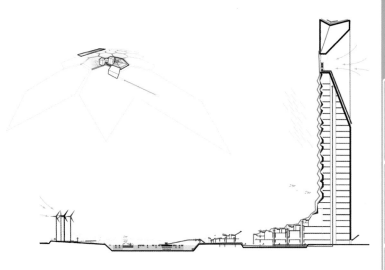

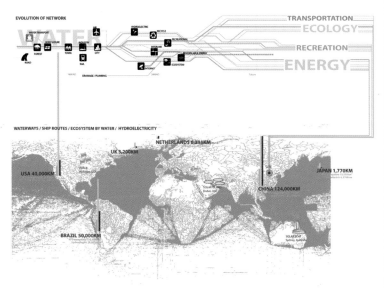

EVOLUTION OF NETWORK

WATER

TRANSPORTATION
ECOLOGY
RECREATION
ENERGY

WATERWAYS / SHIP ROUTES / ECOSYSTEM BY WATER / HYDROELECTRICITY

NETHERLANDS 6,211KM

UK 3,200KM

USA 40,000KM

JAPAN 1,770KM

CHINA 124,000KM

BRAZIL 50,000KM

LIVING LANDSCAPES

URBAN GREEN

BIO INFRASTRUCTURES

ENERGY SYSTEMS

PARAMETRIC URBANISM

SOCIAL & COLLABORATIVE

THEORIES & STRATEGIES

ABSTRACT CITY: UKRAINE

Kovalyk Ihor
XII

ikovalyk@gmail.com

Ukraine

The self-sufficient city system allows combining infrastructure of a big city with the comfortable natural environment. Idea is to restrict the growth of urban units by wide green lines of natural landscape and agricultural sectors.

It plays the role of protective green areas that hold the shape and the size of urban units without giving them the possibility of uncontrolled spread.

The transport system has several levels of functional and spatial differentiation. City system based on the urban modules structure in the form of artificial plates raised above the ground level and simulating its natural surface. Plates are cuted by the street public chains (channels). On the surface of the plates there are residential buildings in a shape of cone-hills which are formed by descending spiral green terraces. Residential buildings act as energy receivers.

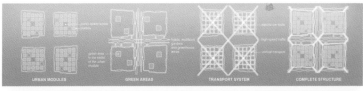

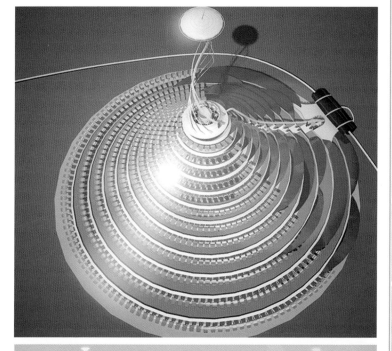

LIVING LANDSCAPES

URBAN GREEN

BIO INFRASTRUCTURES

ENERGY SYSTEMS

PARAMETRIC URBANISM

SOCIAL & COLLABORATIVE

THEORIES & STRATEGIES

horizontal air movement

UPDRAFT EFFECT

This air inside the building will warm up as a result of the operation of the industrial system. Inflow of external such air will create a powerful updraft which will become a wind plant in the upper narrow part of the building.

COLLECTING WATER

Buildings collecting water from the rain and from the ground. Rainwater collector is set up along the spiral terraces. It collects rainwater. Due to the slope of the terraces the water from the whole building surface naturally runs through the collector and is accumulated in a tank. This collector gets water to the bottom of the structure. There are turbines along the whole length of the collector which produce electricity during the rain.

LIVING LANDSCAPES

URBAN GREEN

BIO-INFRASTRUCTURES

ENERGY SYSTEMS

PARAMETRIC URBANISM

SOCIAL & COLLABORATIVE

THEORIES & STRATEGIES

THE CITY POWER OF 10

Melman Joachim
Maignial Benoit
Simon G. Phelipot
Honffo William

joachim.melman@gmail.com

France

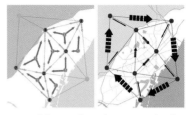

More than an architectural approach the project is a key method based on 3 concepts; social flux hub, urban agriculture, advanced energy loop.

Aimed to be developped throughout three different time scale; diagnostic (0 year), healing town(10 years), catalysing (100 years), the main act consists in rethinking urban transports exchanges, thus permitting a usefull land reorganisation of the streets (urban agriculture). A new type of aerial public transport megafast and green is linking the sensitive areas of the city throughout vertical multi functions beacons. The vertical multi modal axes being the convergence point of the traffic flux receive a number of citizen functions, as cultural places, meeting places, civic functions, markets points, but also alternative energy solutions.

The final output is to catalyse; social net hub, increasing civic life, metropolitain ecosystems, urban agriculture, local and global transport, energy loop and to provide great life style.

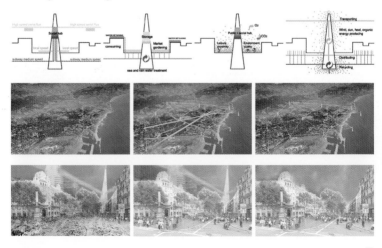

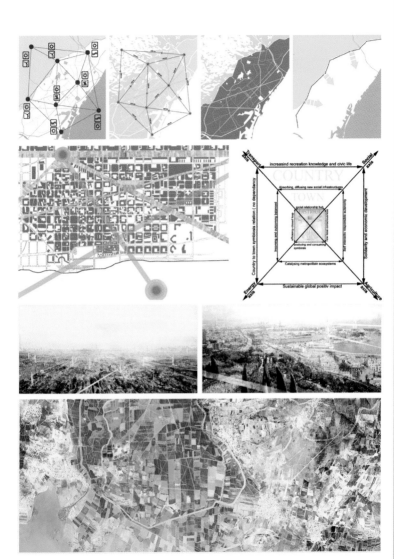

LIVING LANDSCAPES

URBAN GREEN

BIO INFRASTRUCTURES

ENERGY SYSTEMS

PARAMETRIC URBANISM

SOCIAL & COLLABORATIVE

THEORIES & STRATEGIES

COUNTRY TOWN

increasind recreation knowledge and civic life

Absorbing, diffusing new social infrastructures

social relationship hub

Country to town symbiosis relation (no dependancy

Boosting autonomia balanced

efficiency closed loop

Self esteeme responsible autonomy

Revolving and consuming symbiosis

Catalysing metropolitain ecosystems

Sustainable global positiv impact

Transport axis

Social axis

Energy axis

Agriculture axis

Solidarity and economic development

FoMC - FIELDS OF METABOLIC CLEANSERS

Shroff Kayzad
Maria Isabel Jimenez Leon

k.shroff@shroffleon.com

India

The scheme proposes to piggy back the function of the park with that of an urban metabolic cleanser, collecting the sewage from the immediate context and recycling it through ecological means, using root zone treatments, into usable water.
The scheme utilizes an ecological cleansing prototype having a capacity of accommodating 60.000 Liters/Day, as the global ordering element. 146 such prototypes are proliferated across the site in regions that accommodate for it's natural tendency, which in totality administers the purification of approximately 9,000,000l of sewage a day, roughly 3% of the total sewage production of Quito.
In distributing the prototypes, with their multiple sub parts, each revealing its own sensibility of scale and materiality, the site inherits a structural skeleton; that is both performative its in nature and intrinsic to the terrain of the existing topography. Using the distribution array as a defining framework, the site is then infused with secondary functions of the park – greens, paths etc...

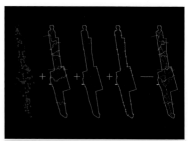

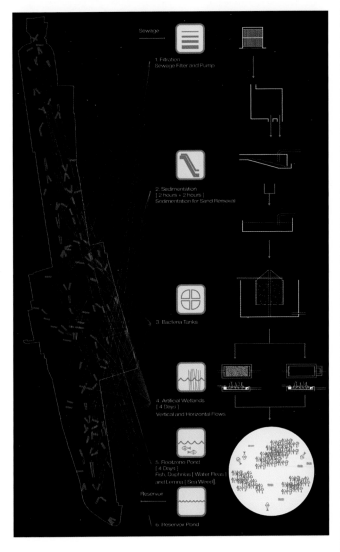

Sewage →

1. Filtration
Sewage Filter and Pump

2. Sedimentation
[2 hours + 2 hours]
Sedimentation for Sand Removal

3. Bacteria Tanks

4. Artificial Wetlands
[4 Days]
Vertical and Horizontal Flows

5. Rootzone Pond
[4 Days]
Fish, Duphinus | Water Fleas
and Lemna | Sea Weed].

Reservoir →

6. Reservoir Pond

LIVING LANDSCAPES

URBAN GREEN

BIO-INFRASTRUCTURES

ENERGY SYSTEMS

PARAMETRIC URBANISM

SOCIAL & COLLABORATIVE

THEORIES & STRATEGIES

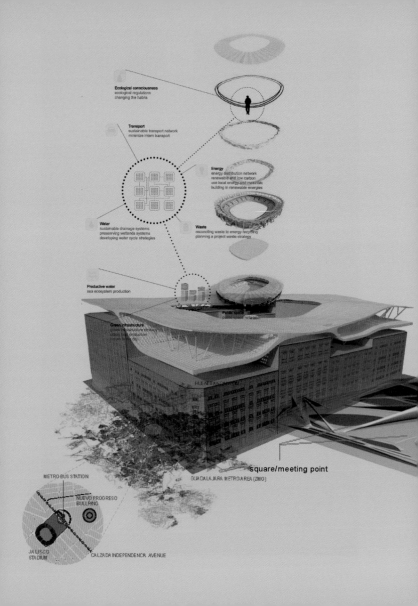

Ecological consciousness
ecological regulations
changing the habits

Transport
sustainable transport network
minimize intern transport

Energy
energy distribution network
renewable and low carbon
use local energy and materials
building in renewable energies

Water
sustainable drainage systems
preserving wetlands systems
developing water cycle strategies

Waste
reconciling waste to energy recycling
planning a project waste strategy

Productive water
sea ecosystem production

Green infrastructure

Public space

square/meeting point

GUADALAJARA METRO AREA (ZMG)

METROBUS STATION

NUEVO PROGRESO
BULLRING

JALISCO
STADIUM

CALZADA INDEPENDENCIA AVENUE

URBAN GREEN

LIVING LANDSCAPES

URBAN GREEN

BIO-INFRASTRUCTURES

ENERGY SYSTEMS

PARAMETRIC URBANISM

SOCIAL & COLLABORATIVE

THEORIES & STRATEGIES

waste wa...
supply sy

orchard park farm

...lation

URBAN GREEN

The city as we know it today is something totally different from the first urban settlements of human beings. Over the years, not only the form of the city but also its systems of organization and functional networks have been developed and transformed.

When we observe the cycle of life and the transfer of energy in Nature, we can see that each member of the natural environment not only consumes but also contributes equal quantities of energy. It seems that this balance has been upset by all our forms of urban organization. The city acts like a parasite, growing and being transformed over the years, taking advantage of all of the energies Nature provides without giving anything back in return.

It is high time we reconsidered not only the way the city is organized but also the way it functions. All forms of urban organization should stop acting against the natural environment which hosts them. The 'Urban Green' category presents all of the projects that have tried to develop proposals in which the urban environment can co-exist effectively and harmoniously along with the natural environment.

Various ways of accomplishing this goal are presented here. It might seem that the urban environment could provide the basis on which to develop a new natural environment. However, this would result in the co-existence of two different layers, and although the living conditions of the city would become better and healthier, the two environments would not really be collaborating and interacting. Taking this approach a step further, the projects presented here proposed a total re-organization of the city's systems and functional networks.

The city, considered as an organism, must change the way it metabolizes the energy it consumes and the energy it puts back into the environment. The redefinition of the functional networks of the city is perceived as vital in enabling the city to become a significant part of the natural cycle of life and the transfers of energy that constantly take place within it.

The creation of new cyclical ecological processes is something more than architecture: it is about defining new functional systems and developing new habits, while at the same time embracing our environmental responsibilities.

LIVING LANDSCAPES

URBAN GREEN

BIO INFRASTRUCTURES

ENERGY SYSTEMS

PARAMETRIC URBANISM

SOCIAL & COLLABORATIVE

THEORIES & STRATEGIES

SELF-EQUIPPED BE A PLEASING PLACE TO ING

Albaladejo Aparicio Pablo

palbalad@hotmail.com

Spain

The trident shaped garden is part of the historic Real place of Aranjuez.
It's necessary to revitalize this residual space, incorporating it to the city, and creating a new scene in the landscape.
It's proposed a Workshop School program mixed whit an attraction focus for the city: An activities attractor and a creator of job.
The park will be like an alive entity in constant growth, fed thanks to its own activities and jobs.

The project was born from a sense development, approaching to a human scale, thinking to be walked in lot of ways.
It offers a lot of interesting spatial and functional connections: a system of 'topographic games'.
The students will use the spare materials to build and change the park, so it can be called a SELF·EQUIPED PARK.

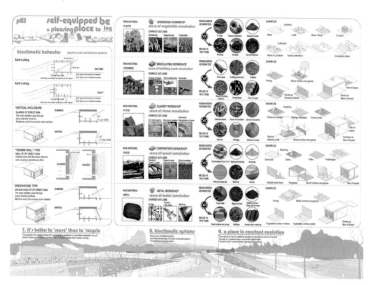

94

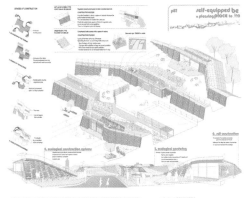

KEYWORDS

— multifunctional equipped park
— regeneration of residual places
— ecological construction systems and gardening
— self construction
— 'reuse' vs 'recycle'
— bioclimatic systems
— a place in constant evolution

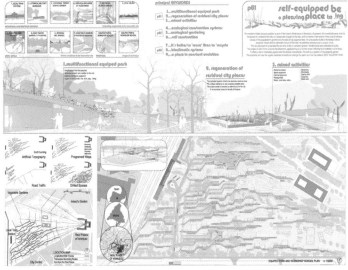

LIVING LANDSCAPES

URBAN GREEN

BIOINFRASTRUCTURES

ENERGY SYSTEMS

PARAMETRIC URBANISM

SOCIAL & COLLABORATIVE

THEORIES & STRATEGIES

FITTING SYSTEMS

Ruiz Gimenez Marta
Marin Eduard
Cesc Massanas Van de Ven
Jordi Pimàs Megias

m.rz.gmz@gmail.com

Spain

To transform our Super-Dependent System into a high-grade Self-Sufficient one, we'll have to fit its total ecological footprint into the area considered part of our system. The strategy brings in to two basic solutions:

A_reduce the ecological footprint
ECOLOGICAL CONSCIOUSNESS
A rational ecological consciousness would reduce the footprint, within it's limits, much faster than anything.

URBAN STRATEGIES
As it can be seen on the graphics, our power to reduce the ecological footprint is mostly reserved on the CO_2 absorption area: energy, transport, waste and water. A NODAL URBAN STRATEGY would reduce traffic necessities, renewable energies would replace the unsustainable ones, and recycling would transform waste into resources.

B_increase system's surface
INCREASE SYSTEM'S SURFACE
Letting the city grow on it's vertical axis generates a more compact city, consuming less space, reducing the internal traffic, and giving the city new spaces to produce resources, which at the same time will decrease it's internal dependence, producing an unpolarized urban plan, organized in hight self-sufficient index nodes.

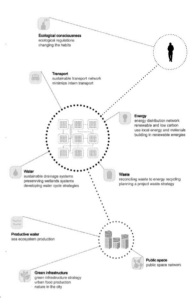

96

LIVING LANDSCAPES

URBAN GREEN

BIO INFRASTRUCTURES

ENERGY SYSTEMS

PARAMETRIC URBANISM

SOCIAL & ECO-COLLABORATIVE

THEORIES & STRATEGIES

self-sufficiency

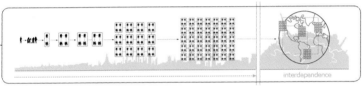

interdependence

ecological footprint

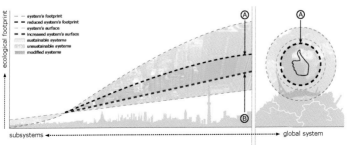

LIVING LANDSCAPES

URBAN GREEN

BIO-INFRASTRUCTURES

ENERGY SYSTEMS

PARAMETRIC URBANISM

SOCIAL & COLLABORATIVE

THEORIES & STRATEGIES

MOBILIZING VILLAGE

Trung Kien Do

dtk_kts@yahoo.com

Vietnam

The idea is how to create a cheap floating community in which it is self-supported and its "cell" can be mobilized and adapt easily with new environment, new location or new timeline. It also can allow other components to join in and out to create more functions of living.

By setting up a hexagonal grid, that will allow adaptation and multiple of housing. Individual house can be joined easily with the other ones to create a "mobilizing community", on one hand; this community is really suitable with nomadic living culture of local fishermen. On the other hand, grouping together can provide more space for food productivity, social activities or playground for children as well. Each module can be designed as a house, a farm, a pond even a library, a school or a clinic. The mobilized school can "feed" all needed and give them a flexible time to attend that only way to attract children. Similarly, community centre or medical care can be transferred from one community to other and provides occupants all essences they need. The form of the house is similar to a carving rock, inspired from natural islands on the bay that makes the village very integrated and distinctive. The cone shape is twisted by a diagonal structure to make the house really resistant with severe weather

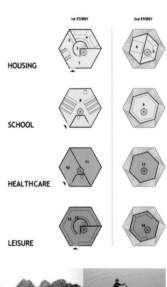

LIVING LANDSCAPES

URBAN GREEN

BIO-INFRASTRUCTURES

ENERGY SYSTEMS

PARAMETRIC URBANISM

SOCIAL & COLLABORATIVE

THEORIES & STRATEGIES

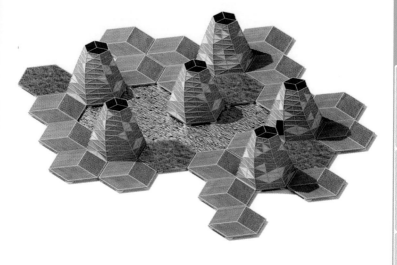

LIVING LANDSCAPES

URBAN GREEN

BIO INFRASTRUCTURES

ENERGY SYSTEMS

PARAMETRIC URBANISM

SOCIAL & COLLABORATIVE

THEORIES & STRATEGIES

CLOUD GARDEN

Kress Benjamin
Cristina Barron Vaquero
benjamin.kress@gmx.net

Spain

TRANSFORMING EXISTING CITY STRUCTURES

"The wooded and hilly city.
I imagine streets covered completely
with forests, so that you can walk from
the street over the wooded hills. In fact
you are walking over the houses."
Hundertwasser

BARRIO SALAMANCA

Speculation transformed the initial ideas
for the district, creating high density
blocks with minimal inner patios. This creates a lack of public green spaces, such
as social facilities and it produces climatic
and environmental problems.

LIVING LANDSCAPES

URBAN GREEN

BIO INFRASTRUCTURES

ENERGY SYSTEMS

PARAMETRIC URBANISM

SOCIAL & COLLABORATIVE

THEORIES & STRATEGIES

CLOUDGARDEN

A net leaf project, falling on the city, slightly posing hardly touching the buildings. Shaping itself in order to fit the different heights. Creating a landscape on the top with public facilities in spaces between. Acting as a buffer for the hard climate conditions of Madrid.

"Rooftops are places to be conquered. Discovering new spaces for and in the city, where it is possible to innovate. In built-up environments, places that enjoys the conditions of light, ventilation and views that are characteristic of environments further from the centre."
Hak Nam

FARM CITY

Capillé Cauê Costa

cauecapille@gmail.com

Brazil

From paleotechnic to biotechnic Cities

from paleotechnic to biotechnic cities

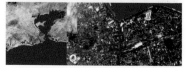

The city of Rio de Janeiro, as many other cities in the world, has grown up in the XIX century following a transport system based on the train line. Train and tram made a 6 km city transform into a 300 km metropolis. In the first decades of the XX century, cars had appeared in Rio. Before the 80's, lots of big highways expand Rio even more. Now, 10 million people live in this 40km wide metropolis. Lots of big problems come from this super sized city: transportation, housing, pollution, poverty, food distribution... Focusing in the food distribution, we can see the amount of problems: food is produced more than 50km away from the city center; it is transported in trucks which pollute the air and waste more than a half of the food produced; after that, it is sold in big markets that waste a little more; the consumer eats it at home and put it packages and leftovers in the same trash; this trash is taken to a big sanitary landfilll near the food production...

How can we solve this problem? How can we stop this one way (paleotechnic) system and transform it into a cycle ("biotechnic") web that pollute less, waste less and spend less? How can our metropolis become self suffient in terms of food?

LIVING LANDSCAPES
URBAN GREEN
BIO INFRASTRUCTURES
ENERGY SYSTEMS
PARAMETRIC URBANISM
SOCIAL & COLLABORATIVE
THEORIES & STRATEGIES

A metropolitan scale problem needs a metropolitan scale solution

To understand a problem, it is necessary to understand its scale. This way, to change a metropolitan production-distribution-consuming of food, we need to act in a metropolitan scale. So garden farming is a nice action, but a house is only a cell in the urban body. We need to act in the park scale, in the school scale, in the train station scale.

This way, we have chosen an abandoned big train station in the heart of Rio downtown to be transformed into an urban "farm-park", which produces, study and sell organic food. This big "farm-park" would be the first of a group of linked urban farms, 10km distant of each other.

To understand a problem, it is necessary to understand its scale. This way, to change a metropolitan production-distribution-consuming of food, we need to act in a metropolitan scale. So garden farming is a nice action, but a house is only a cell in the urban body. We need to act in the park scale, in the school scale, in the train station scale.

This way, we have chosen an abandoned big train station in the heart of Rio downtown to be transformed into an urban "farm-park", which produces, study and sell organic food. This big "farm-park" would be the first of a group of linked urban farms, 10km distant of each other.

a metropolitan scale problem needs
a metropolitan scale solution

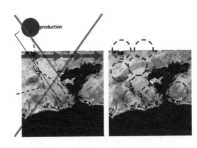

The urban-farm-school-park-market and the environment

The first Urban Farm, besides being also a Park, a School and a big Market, would be an example of good relationship with the surrounding environment:

a) The water comes from rainwater and from the channel near the park.
b) All buildings use a mix of solar and wind energy (roofs are made to provide enough light during all the day, especially in the market).
c) The most important buildings comes from a reuse of old structures of the train station.
d) Workers and students come from surrounding houses.
e) All the food wasted is used as seasoning.

urban-farm-school-park-market

1 green houses* / botanic garden

2 research center / school

3 main entrance

4 market

5 parking (bike and car) / tram station

6 farm*

* The most important production are: tomatoes, potatoes, aipim, carrot, beetroot, onions, garlic, ginger, lettuce, watercress, rícula, mint, basil, goyaba, apple, pear, banana, coconut, passion fruit, lemon, watermelon, açaí, mamão, maize, avocado, strawberry, pumpkin, pea, beans, rice, lentil, grape, maté, inhame, etc..

The water comes from rainwater and the channel near the park.
All buildings use a mix of solar and wind energy (roofs are made to provide enough light during all the day, especially in the market).
The most important buildings comes from a reuse of old structures of the train station.
Workers and students come from surrounding houses.
All the food wasted is used as seasoning.

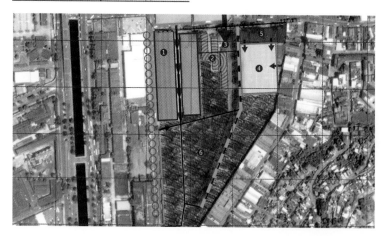

LIVING LANDSCAPES

URBAN GREEN

BIG INFRASTRUCTURES

ENERGY SYSTEMS

PARAMETRIC URBANISM

SOCIAL & COLLABORATIVE

THEORIES & STRATEGIES

Farm cities of today

What results we can expect after the construction of the first urban park-farm?

1. Family and community agriculture diffusion

The idea of a urban farming must be absorbed by the families and communities in the city. The research center / school needs to teach and help people to make their own farm, in their own houses. Besides that, the market may sell tools and pieces of a technological house farm.

2. Reduction of food waste and air pollution (from the unnecessary long distance transportation)

As the production and distribution occur in the same place, all the waste and pollution caused from the long distance transportation is finished.

3. Creation of self sufficient centers (in terms of food) of 10km diameter

The city needs to be a web of farm-parks. This way, this "farm city" would be able to live in a biotechnic system, which would guarantee long and good life to it.
Self sufficiency is a matter of living in a harmonic cycle system.

Alive urbanity

To be alive, the city needs to merge different cultures, functions, spaces, territories, systems, etc.. All this parts needs to be interlaced into a big collage of systems. Each system, however, must be self sufficient – and self suffiency does not come from super neotechnological advances: it comes from the most simple organic system, in other words, a cycle.This way, we can say that a city is alive when all its parts are feeding themselves with their own old structures, as a living forest.

<u>**farm cities of today**</u>

2010 2015 2020 2025 2030 2035 2040 2045 2050 2055 2060 2065 2070 2075 2080 2085

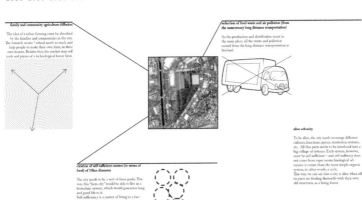

family and community agriculture diffusion

The idea of a urban farming must be absorbed by the families and communities in the city. The research center / school needs to teach and help people to make their own farm, in their own houses. Besides that, the market may sell tools and pieces of a technological house farm.

reduction of food waste and air pollution (from the unnecessary long distance transportation)

As the production and distribution occur in the same place, all the waste and pollution caused from the long distance transportation is finished.

alive urbanity

To be alive, the city needs to merge different cultures, functions, spaces, territories, systems, etc.. All this parts needs to be interlaced into a big collage of systems. Each system, however, must be self sufficient – and self suffiency does not come from super neotechnological advances: it comes from the most simple organic system, in other words, a cycle.This way, we can say that a city is alive when all its parts are feeding themselves with their own old structures, as a living forest.

creation of self sufficient centers (in terms of food) of 10km diameter

The city needs to be a web of farm-parks. This way, this "farm city" would be able to live in a biotechnic system, which would guarantee long and good life to it.
Self sufficiency is a matter of living in a harmonic cycle system.

RUNNER-UP

MASSIVE URBAN RECYCLING JALISCO STADIUM

Adrian Garcia
Douglas Rodriguez

adriangarciagarcia00@gmail.com

Mexico

The Jalisco Stadium in Guadalajara Mexico is the third largest in the country, with a capacity of 56,713, built in 1690 and participated in the 1970's and 1986's World Cup Soccer, home of the most famous football team, "Chivas Raya-das de Guadalajara", nowadays in the decadence state of his evolution process within the city's timeline. Soon, the construction will be a huge hole on the city volume.

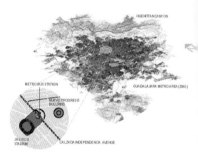

ROOF

The project is about to recycle Jalisco Stadium to create a micro-city, a contained ecosystem, with cyclical ecological processes like water and solar uptake, wastes treatments and temperature regulation. Cities tend to explode; recycling residual space inside the stadium and concentrating its different programmatic functions is an opposite reaction against expansion promoted by the contemporary local urban developers. The city must grow within itself, instead explode and expand. The project works under a very simple principle, filling the blank. Death or evolution of human activities leaves behind apparently useless architecture. The project urbanizes using this iconographic modernism corps, giving it a second chance.

UPPER BOWL CIRCULATIONS

UPPER BOWL HOUSING

LOWER BOWL HOUSING

RECYCLED STRUCTURE

PLAYFIELD

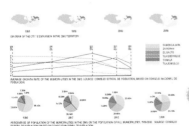

ALL TOGHETER

LIVING LANDSCAPES

URBAN GREEN

BIO INFRASTRUCTURES

ENERGY SYSTEMS

PARAMETRIC URBANISM

SOCIAL & COLLABORATIVE

THEORIES & STRATEGIES

LIVING LANDSCAPES

URBAN GREEN

BIO-INFRASTRUCTURES

ENERGY SYSTEMS

PARAMETRIC URBANISM

SOCIAL & COLLABORATIVE

THEORIES & STRATEGIES

WATER UPTAKE

The enormous roof surface will work as a rain collector, sending water to the tanks and then distributing it to be used for house purposes. The wastewater from houses is treated on the tanks and taken back for toilet drowning and green areas irrigation.

SOLAR ENERGY UPTAKE

Photovoltaic cells are placed all over the roof structure catching almost 365 days of Guadalajara sun, keeping it in batteries for all year energy supply.

TEMPERATURE REGULATION

The building regulates its temperature due to the crossed ventilation between the roof and the upper bowl.

WASTEWATER TREATMENT

Wastewater from houses is treated on artificial filters then taken to the wetlands distributed on the green areas for irrigation; the surplus is filtered to subsoil.

SOLID WASTE TREATMENT

Solid waste is divided for its treatment; organic waste is taken to the compost to be reinstated as fertile soil in the center field and inorganic waste is separated and taken to recycle center placed in the commercial concourse.

Upper bowl circulations are composed by three peripheral rings, one for level, connected to the housing modules.

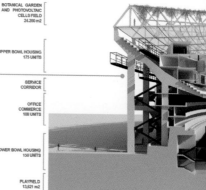

BOTANICAL GARDEN AND PHOTOVOLTAIC CELLS FIELD 24,200 m2

UPPER BOWL HOUSING 175 UNITS

SERVICE CORRIDOR

OFFICE COMMERCE 108 UNITS

LOWER BOWL HOUSING 150 UNITS

PLAYFIELD 13,621 m2

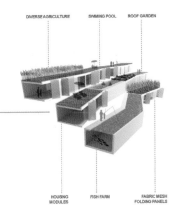

DIVERSE AGRICULTURE   SWIMMING POOL   ROOF GARDEN

HOUSING MODULES   FISH FARM   FABRIC MESH FOLDING PANELS

LIVING LANDSCAPES

URBAN GREEN

BIO INFRASTRUCTURES

ENERGY SYSTEMS

PARAMETRIC URBANISM

SOCIAL & COLLABORATIVE

THEORIES & STRATEGIES

ORCHARD TOWER

De Gregorio Marco

degregoriomarco@gmail.com

Italy

Through digital technique, this project explores the qualities of the Cerdà's grid. The building is conceived as a body-fluid system like the lymphatic, it forms the structure and the spatial configuration of the construction.

On the top of the building there is a rain water tank where the collected water flows through the "veining-structure", serving each floor of the building and providing water for irrigation of the orchard.

The project explores the possibilities of food/farming in an urban context by incorporating a traditional orchard in the city. It reasserts the environmental issues and the sustainable importance of "locally produced food" for the city and for the health of its residents.

Beyond creating a local food source, the notion of urban farming becomes an important resource in supporting the world's food supply.

The residents become both the producers and the consumers of the garden farm products.

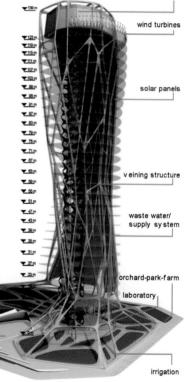

rainwater collector

wind turbines

solar panels

veining structure

waste water/ supply system

orchard-park-farm

laboratory

square/meeting point

irrigation

LIVING LANDSCAPES

URBAN GREEN

BIO/INFRASTRUCTURES

ENERGY SYSTEMS

PARAMETRIC URBANISM

SOCIAL & COLLABORATIVE

THEORIES & STRATEGIES

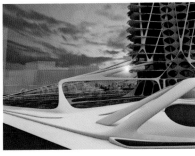

LIVING LANDSCAPES

URBAN GREEN

BIO INFRASTRUCTURES

ENERGY SYSTEMS

PARAMETRIC URBANISM

SOCIAL & COLLABORATIVE

THEORIES & STRATEGIES

GREEN TRANSPLANT

Termote Delphine

delphine.termote@gmail.com

Belgium

"Green transplant" draws the main lines of a new urban approach applying an ecological layer on the actual city. It points up a series of strategies rather than a way of making architecture, according to the fact that sustainable building considers the city's parameters. Five different rules were so developed to work in complementary fashion : rebuilding the sustainable city on the city, establishing a positif meshing in order to restore the energic balance, sliding back the current cycle, applying bioclimatic constructive principles and finally including the citizen in this action to achieve a real change of consumption habits.

Brussels was choosen as a case study to apply and verify the line attack. In this city the process would take about 40 years to manage the transformation of the actual city into a self-sufficient city thanks to the developpement of 18 impact points of various scales in centra nurbs of the city.

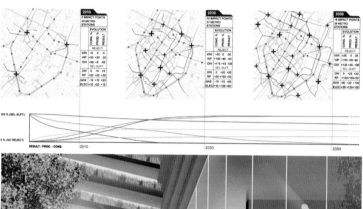

LIVING LANDSCAPES

URBAN GREEN

BIO INFRASTRUCTURES

ENERGY SYSTEMS

PARAMETRIC URBANISM

SOCIAL & COLLABORATIVE

THEORIES & STRATEGIES

West

South

East

North

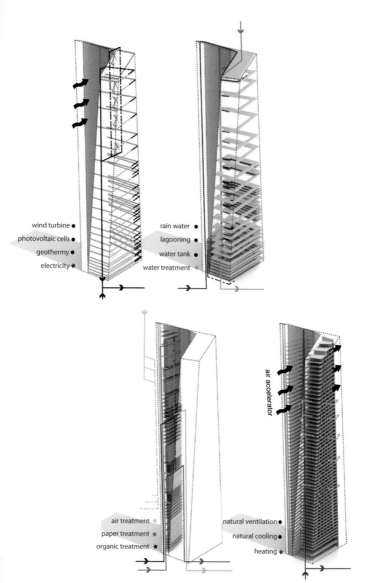

wind turbine ●
photovoltaic cells ●
geothermy ●
electricity ★

rain water ●
lagooning ●
water tank ●
water treatment ★

air treatment ●
paper treatment ★
organic treatment ★

air accelerator

natural ventilation ●
natural cooling ●
heating ★

LIVING LANDSCAPES

URBAN GREEN

BIO INFRASTRUCTURES

ENERGY SYSTEMS

PARAMETRIC URBANISM

SOCIAL & COLLABORATIVE

THEORIES & STRATEGIES

LIFELINE

Diamond Geoffrey
Robert Benson
Lisa Ekle
Brian Vitale

geoff@eightwest.com

United States

Our societal challenges are too significant, and the potential of the Bloomingdale Line in Chicago too great, for it to be solely another park or workout regimen as it has been presupposed by many. The long-abandoned and currently derelict viaduct should be put to a use with greater purpose, one that will directly affect the people most in need within the City. It must be transformed into a great producer, and a great landmark for Chicago - a highly visible greenhouse with a hydrogen production system and storage tank tucked safely within the line's existing mass, both of which rely solely on the sun and water as their sources of fuel.

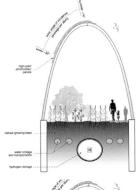

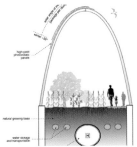

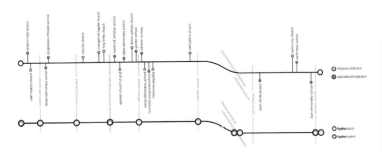

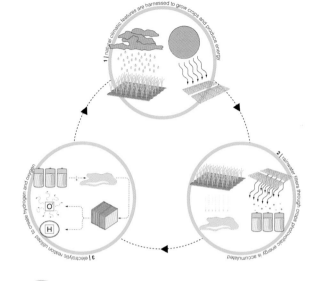

1 | natural climatic features are harnessed to grow crops and produce energy

2 | rainwater filters through crops providing energy is accumulated

3 | electrolytic reaction utilized to create hydrogen and pure oxygen

O

H

H

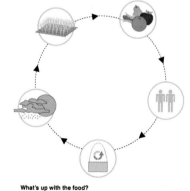

What happens to all that hydrogen?
We've been busy making gobs of hydrogen. We've been even busier deciding what to do with it all. When lifeline has completed the electrolysis process, effectively splitting water into hydrogen and pure oxygen, it's time to put the good stuff to use. lifeline creates more than enough hydrogen to power any nearby schools and churches as well as depots at key intersections along the Line where hydrogen-powered vehicles can 'gas' up with our cleaner, healthier fuel.

What's up with the food?
So, we're making hydrogen and growing crops all at the same time. Well, actually, we're using the crops to produce the hydrogen and we're using the hydrogen to produce the crops. Still with us? Good. If there's one thing that a city the size of Chicago needs as desperately as clean energy and a healthier environment, it's food. Finding ten acres of potable soil in the heart of a dense urban environment is no easy task, but, we've managed to do just that.

LIVING LANDSCAPES

URBAN GREEN

BIO-INFRASTRUCTURES

ENERGY SYSTEMS

PARAMETRIC URBANISM

SOCIAL & COLLABORATIVE

THEORIES & STRATEGIES

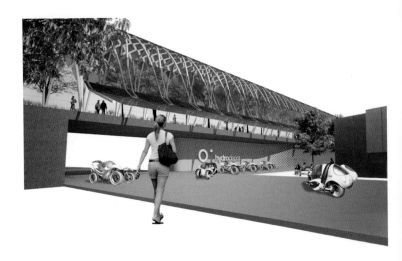

wAs the system produces this much needed food and energy, it releases clean oxygen as the only by-product of hydrogen production and photosynthesis - a truly sustainable loop.

At three miles long, the greenhouse will be a visual marker, both day and night, and a symbol of hope and conscious commitment for Chicago. It will have nearly ten acres of land to farm year-round, producing enough food to supplement the Greater Food Depository of Chicago's resources to feed

those in need (which by last count was an astonishing 500,000 adults and children in Cook County alone). The remaining forty percent of the yield will be sold at strategically located markets throughout the line's diverse neighborhoods.

The hydrogen generator below the greenhouse uses a nano-photovoltaic curtain to create the electricity required to split the water (H_2O) molecules into pure Hydrogen (H) and Oxygen (O). The Hydrogen is stored in tanks while the Oxygen is released into the atmosphere

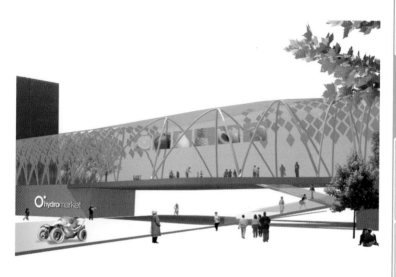

LIVING LANDSCAPES

URBAN GREEN

BIO-INFRASTRUCTURES

ENERGY SYSTEMS

PARAMETRIC URBANISM

SOCIAL & COLLABORATIVE

THEORIES & STRATEGIES

– rehabilitating our increasingly damaged supply. The new fuel cell energy (our stored hydrogen) will be used to power nearby Chicago Public Schools and places of worship. The public school system can begin to reverse its budget shortfall from last year - which amounted to teacher layoffs as the result of rising utility bills. Hydrogen equals teachers.

Finally, the excess Hydrogen will be sold to alternative fuel vehicles at depots located at major terrestrial intersections along the line. The waste of these vehicles is water, which can be stored in the vehicles and returned to the lifeline system to again feed the production of hydrogen and thus continue the loop.

The lifeline system must stand as a symbol for a new future; a new paradigm that involves examining abandoned and under utilized infrastructure for new energy bearing potentials. Locally produced, cleaner energy means a healthier and more stable society.

This is the catalyst. This is the lifeline.

BAUCI 2040

Servi Lorenzo

info@serraglia.com

Italia

The illegal management of waste is concentrated in the area between three cities close by Naples: Acerra, Nola and Marigliano.

The waste management technique is very simple: when a dump is getting full, it is burned. This is why the area is sadly nick-named "the land of fires" by Roberto Saviano in the best seller book "Gomorra". This area was one of the most fertile land in all Italy. Nowadays, the situation is dramatic: the ground contains very high levels of toxic elements as copper, arsenic, mercury and PCBs. The land is contaminated as well as the air. Agriculture is on the decline and the health risks are rising.

Latest studies by The Lancet Oncology shows how liver tumours are increasing.

Bauci is a gesture of love from citizens of Naples area. The citizens are extremely upset and worried about the dire condition of their own land. Thus, they decided to move and to live above it. In this way the land is free to relax from its environmental stress. Bauci is a temporary network-city for about 100.000 habitants. Bauci interacts only selectively with the outside environment. The small footprint of the new city doesn't tax the host area. It is self-sustaining city. It grows its own food, it requires no resources from the host area and it recycles all of its waste.

The network is constituted from three types of cities: the living city, where people live in a child-friendly urban environment with green areas and no cars.

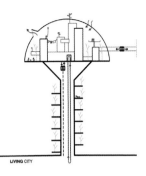

LIVING CITY

the recycling city, where people work in recycling and waste managing. Here is recycled all the waste from the living and agriculture cities. All the waste is recycled and transformed in re usable products.

Most of the material is used in Bauci. In addition, extra production (e.g. energy) is sold to other cities. The reclycling city is also filtering outside air. The agriculture city, where people cultivate fruit and vegetables in crop rotation. The products are used in Bauci and the extra yield is sold to local markets. The goal is that the host land will restore its natural environment and one day people can return to live in the land with a more sustainable style of life.

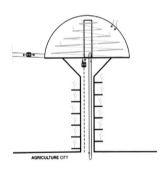

AGRICULTURE CITY

NOLA

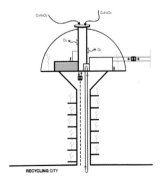

RECYCLING CITY

LIVING LANDSCAPES

URBAN GREEN

BIO INFRASTRUCTURES

ENERGY SYSTEMS

PARAMETRIC URBANISM

SOCIAL & COLLABORATIVE

THEORIES & STRATEGIES

LIVING LANDSCAPES

URBAN GREEN

BIO-INFRASTRUCTURES

ENERGY SYSTEMS

PARAMETRIC URBANISM

SOCIAL & COLLABORATIVE

THEORIES & STRATEGIES

THE AGRARIAN FIELD
+ FIELD LANDSCAPE

Jennifer Daniels

jennifer.c.daniels@gmail.com

United States

The Problem:

The increase of population - a strong argument for urban living- has required 1.2 acres of farmland per average person (to sustain dietary requirements). In addition, the equivalent to 1 acre is lost per person increase in population. This consumption of land will result in the devastation of arable land by 2050. What is the resolution? Can farm and city intersect? Can there be efficiency in this intersection?

The categorization of program is not efficient unless each category can co-exist symbiotically. Two programs of function have fluctuated severely in opposing trends: agriculture and technology. By the 2050, the ratio of arable land to population for the US alone will be a third of what they were at the beginning of the century. This will have a severe impact on the landscape and diplomacy of programs.

The Proposal:

The City as a field project explores the compacting capabilities of a city. The very nature of an urban environment pushes the limits of density and necessity. Through its evolution, the city will be required to understand the limits of

EPS PODIUM: floor 4

— rooftop terrace

— lightwell grid

EPS PODIUM: floor 3

— commercial & public opportunity: excess and undefined space gives possibility for future growth and needs

— observation deck: for viewing and education of EPS (energy production system)

— field as EXPERIENCE

— layered hydroponic agriculture: each layer holds crops capable of growing with artificial light and monitored nutrients and water

EPS PODIUM: floor 2

— public bubble: contains interior and exterior program to enhance culture and community

— public assembly: public bubble specially equipped for specific gatherings
— algae collection: wide scrapers gather growing algae from underneath hydroponic crops
— field as EXPERIENCE: landscape is for enjoyment

EPS PODIUM: floor 1

— virtual arcade: access to multimedia interaction

— core circulation: located at 4 corners, provides movement opportunities to all levels

— algae energy converters: transforms algae into useable energy for the city

— generator / energy retention & storage: holds excess energy and food

LIVING LANDSCAPES

URBAN GREEN

BIO-INFRASTRUCTURES

ENERGY SYSTEMS

PARAMETRIC URBANISM

SOCIAL & COLLABORATIVE

THEORIES & STRATEGIES

space, and re-determine its value and function. Through advanced development in technology, plants will grow at a high efficiency rate, with little demand on resources. Through the use of hydroponic gardening, crops can grow up to 10 times the volume per space at the beginning of the 21st century. This method needs to be exploited as a means to limit space as our main resource.

Through the use of stacked hydroponic gardening, algae will opportunistically grow underneath each layer from build-up of water, carbon dioxide, minerals and light. The algae will then be harvested to produce much needed biofuel for the city. The amount of algae needed to equal the amount of diesel consumed in the United States is equal to 0.5% of the farm land used in the country. By 2050, algae will be required to provide most, if not all, of all fuel consumed, and will be economically resilient.

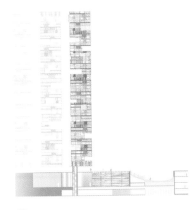

PROGRAM - DUALITIES
PERMACULTURE
— permanent agriculture: agriculture maximized: this stratified environment will optimize the growth of hydroponic plants, requiring only a film of nutrients and water and controlled light.
— permanent culture: agriculture as field, experience. The occupation of a "natural" landscape creates a redefined "American" experience.

TECHNOCULTURE
— Technology as agriculture: stacked vegetation allows the formation and harvesting of algae. The algae is decomposed into energy, that is capable of providing for the city
— Energy Production System: EPS
— Technology as culture: education and information continues to push the 21st century.

FLEXI-COMPACT
— Residential units are compacted to minimize total conditioned space.
—units can expand per specific use of each household. Air space can be occupied for defined amounts of time, creating dynamic boundaries and interactions within a community

Expand-able residential units:
Apartments slide out to accommodate the shifting needs of the tenant, allowing full maximization of AIR SPACE during every moment. This additional space is rented out hourly, or per day, and retracts back into the main core once the space is no longer needed.

SLOPSCRAPER: DIRTY TECH FOR THE CLEAN CITY OF TOMORROW

Southern John
Andrew Alcala

john@urban-ops.net

United States

Slopscraper does not aspire to be architecture. Instead, it cloaks itself in the gaudy trappings of "heavy tech" and functional formalism, supplanting itself into the vertical clutter of today's bustling metropolis as both an object and as a machine. Technically advanced and formally efficient, Slopscraper composts millions of tons of organic waste per year and provides ample fertilizer for the communal gardens of the self-sustaining city of tomorrow.

Slopscraper transgresses decay by presenting the process of putrification in a pleasant-looking, and technologically performative wrapper. Its flexible skin expands as the composting process renders trash into "gardener's gold", keeping the building's shape in constant formal fluctuation as pockets of gas and moisture migrate around the rotting matter inside the structure. Eventually, as the shear organic fertility of Slopscraper pollinates the surrounding neighborhoods, the entire city will become a bountiful garden, ready for life in the self-sustaining city of tomorrow.

LIVING LANDSCAPES

URBAN GREEN

BIO INFRASTRUCTURES

ENERGY SYSTEMS

PARAMETRIC URBANISM

SOCIAL & COLLABORATIVE

THEORIES & STRATEGIES

Power: Hot air generated by the composting process is used to power a central turbine on the roof, which provides power for the project, as well as the surrounding neighborhood.

Aeration: Fans at multiple levels pull in fresh air from the outside and grey-water is recycled from moisture generated by the decomposition process. These are circulated through the core in order to speed up the composting process.

Transport: Compostable trash is brought into the tower and dumped into garbage scows, which take the raw organic material up to the top of the facility for distribution.

Formal Mutation:
As the composted waste decomposes, the gasses and shifting organic matter cause the flexible skin of the building to warp and fold, producing a variety of exciting formal manifestations.

Delivery: Fresh compost spills out of the base of the structure, filling the streets with a fertile topography to be collected by the populace.

Power: Methane generated from the decomposition process is collected and processed in order to provide power for the building, as well as the surrounding neighborhood.

GREEN CITY

Detcheverry Karine

kdetcheverry@free.fr

Canada

To design the city of the future, we have several options:

Transforming rooftops into airborne gardens: Green rooftops are still quite rare in urban areas; polyvalent plantation could be suggested systematically for all high rise projects.

Transforming boulevards into parks or gardens: In the near future, some cities will opt for non-polluting streetcars and computerized share taxis will become commonplace.

Transforming state housing into a source of energy: New generation photovoltaic solar panels are cropping up fast.

Prospects for organic solar cells are very promising: In the near future, we can imagine that it will be technically possible to produce a highly efficient flexible translucide photovoltaic veil allowing for both visibility and an esthetic appearance. We can also imagine an automated waste conveyor system for recycling and waste disposal.

Each urban waste separation collector would be computerized so as to optimize three-category waste separation equipped with a scan system to analyze the waste collector's content prior to transportation through an automated conveyor system.

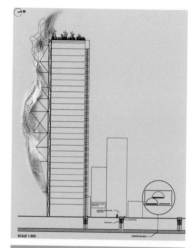

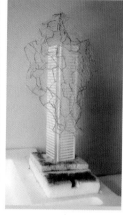

LIVING LANDSCAPES

URBAN GREEN

BIO INFRASTRUCTURES

ENERGY SYSTEMS

PARAMETRIC URBANISM

SOCIAL & COLLABORATIVE

THEORIES & STRATEGIES

LIVING LANDSCAPES

URBAN GREEN

BIO-INFRASTRUCTURES

ENERGY SYSTEMS

PARAMETRIC URBANISM

SOCIAL & COLLABORATIVE

THEORIES & STRATEGIES

MELBOURNE 2030

Dragomir Laurie

laurence@kerstinthompson.com

Australia

PARTIAL OR TOTAL RE-DESIGN?

Architecture widens every physical environment which entours human life; it is composed by modifications and alterations introduced in the surface, terrestrial by now, in order to satisfy what human need. According to this, the re-design of one half, the natural settings. Intelligence artificial capsule Individual units able to receive comings, processing such perceptions and acting consequently, in order to enable goings. It acts in a rational and adequate way, tending to maximize the expected result, according to the user's necessities. It becomes therefore in an attached element, also useful as a means of transport.

SKIN FACADE

The skin composed by lunar fiber perpendicular to the façade's plans allows not only light adaptation and regulation but also able to perspire and heat.

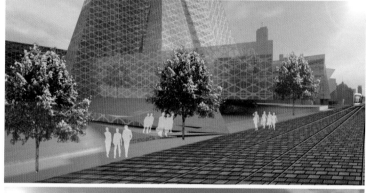

LIVING LANDSCAPES

URBAN GREEN

BIG INFRASTRUCTURES

ENERGY SYSTEMS

PARAMETRIC URBANISM

SOCIAL & COLLABORATIVE

THEORIES & STRATEGIES

LIVING LANDSCAPES

URBAN GREEN

BIO INFRASTRUCTURES

ENERGY SYSTEMS

PARAMETRIC URBANISM

SOCIAL & COLLABORATIVE

THEORIES & STRATEGIES

NATURAL TALENT

LV Haonan

lv_haonan@yahoo.com.cn

China

Cities were originated by the natural environment and showed its appearance thousands of years ago. In a long time the relationship between city and nature has been one of balance.

Urbanism has overtaken nature in the form of a "concrete forrest", conquesting without regard for what the earth left for us to make our living. As cities become bigger and much more complicated, crisis like environment deterioration, shortage of natural resource are not easy to deal with.

We believe it is much more important to think about the relationship between city and nature than to solve problems one by one technically. So the self-sufficient city for us is trying to discover and penetrate into the "natural talent" to seek for solutions systematically.

The proposal aims at reducing energy consumption and increasing production through a "NATURAL TALENTED" way.

Here are the **Key Concepts:**

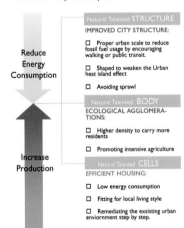

Natural Talented **STRUCTURE**

IMPROVED CITY STRUCTURE:

☐ Proper urban scale to reduce fossil fuel usage by encouraging walking or public transit.

☐ Shaped to weaken the Urban heat island effect

☐ Avoiding sprawl

Natural Talented **BODY**

ECOLOGICAL AGGLOMERA-TIONS:

☐ Higher density to carry more residents

☐ Promoting intensive agriculture

Natural Talented **CELLS**

EFFICIENT HOUSING:

☐ Low energy consumption

☐ Fitting for local living style

☐ Remediating the existing urban enviornment step by step.

Reduce Energy Consumption

Increase Production

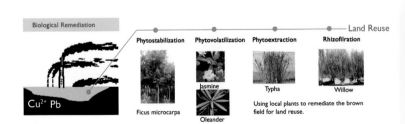

Biological Remediation — Land Reuse

Cu^{2+} Pb

Phytostabilization

Ficus microcarpa

Phytovolatilization

Jasmine

Oleander

Phytoextraction

Typha

Rhizofilration

Willow

Using local plants to remediate the brown field for land reuse.

LIVING LANDSCAPES

URBAN GREEN

BIO INFRASTRUCTURES

ENERGY SYSTEMS

PARAMETRIC URBANISM

SOCIAL & COLLABORATIVE

THEORIES & STRATEGIES

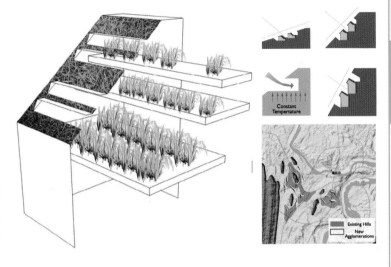

Constant
Temperature

Existing Hills

New
Agglomerations

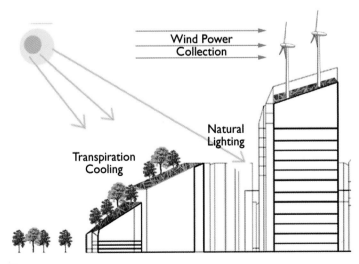

Wind Power
Collection

Natural
Lighting

Transpiration
Cooling

LIVING LANDSCAPES

URBAN GREEN

BIO INFRASTRUCTURES

ENERGY SYSTEMS

PARAMETRIC URBANISM

SOCIAL & COLLABORATIVE

THEORIES & STRATEGIES

CITY AND COUNTRY - BSAS 2050

Gabriel Quipildor
Marcelo Savarro
Santiago Albarracín
Hernan Landolfo
Leonardo Merlos

namachgabriel@hotmail.com

Argentina

The construction of artificialityon countryside generate news oppurtinities to develop urbanism. This is the way that begin the mix between city and country Mixture of opposite concepts, that actualized and confront each other each other, give us the opportunity to develop a new urbanism, that value the autosustentability and a new urban life conected to the rural environment

Vertical constructions or towers give us the opportunity of explore in a vertical way, trying to lean on the ground the minimum as possible. In others words, ground floor spaces are extremely minimum, generating less impact on the natural field. At ground level 80% is empty exclusive for crops, and a 20% (city) to buildings. The fillet is extremely important because that is where they cause the production in the city get the character of city self-sufficient.

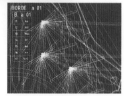

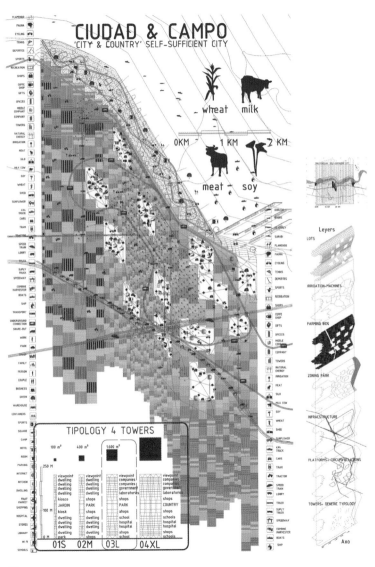

CIUDAD & CAMPO
'CITY & COUNTRY' SELF-SUFFICIENT CITY

wheat milk

0KM — 1 KM — 2 KM

meat — soy

LIVING LANDSCAPES

URBAN GREEN

BIO INFRASTRUCTURES

ENERGY SYSTEMS

PARAMETRIC URBANISM

SOCIAL & COLLABORATIVE

THEORIES & STRATEGIES

Leyers

LOTS

IRRIGATION-MACHINES

FARMING 80%

ZONING PARK

INFRASTRUCTURE

PLATFORMS-CIRCULATIONS

TOWERS- GENERIC TYPOLOGY

Axo

TIPOLOGY 4 TOWERS

100 m²   400 m²   1.600 m²

250 M

01S	02M	03L	04XL
viewpoint	viewpoint	viewpoint	viewpoint
dwelling	dwelling	companies	companies
dwelling	dwelling	government	government
dwelling	dwelling	laboratories	laboratorio
kiosco	shops	shops	shops
JARDIN	PARK	PARK	COUNTRY
kiosk	shops	shops	shops
dwelling	dwelling	school	schools
dwelling	dwelling	hospital	hospital
dwelling	dwelling	hospital	hospital
dwelling	dwelling	shops	shops
park	school	school	schools

100 M

0 M

149

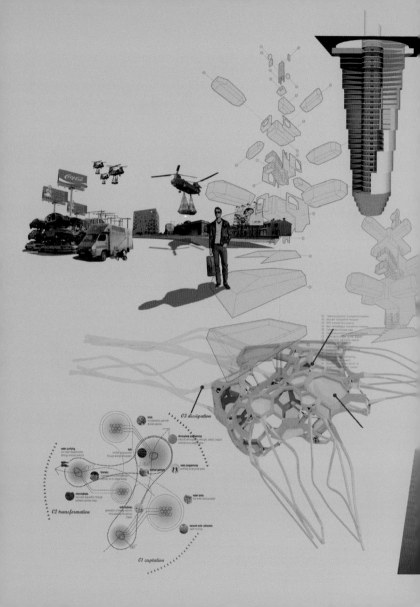

C3 dissipation

C2 transformation

C1 captation

BIO INFRA- STRUC- TURES

LIVING LANDSCAPES

URBAN GREEN

BIO INFRASTRUCTURES

ENERGY SYSTEMS

PARAMETRIC URBANISM

SOCIAL & COLLABORATIVE

THEORIES & STRATEGIES

main structure
18 cm diameter tube

interior skin
ETFE translucent skin

secondary structure
10 cm diameter tube
6 cm diameter tube

exterior skin
ETFE translucent skin

BIO INFRASTRUCTURES

Resources are becoming scarcer by the day, man has upset the balance with his environment, and at every latitude and longitude his settlements are in an unsustainable situation, in a state that cannot be perpetuated indefinitely, inevitably destined to self-destruction in the medium to long term.

In view of our awareness of this grave situation we have to ask ourselves about the existence and feasibility of possible alternative ways of developing human settlements, using solutions that will restore the equilibrium of our cities, in which resources are used but not exploited.

In this state of affairs the self-sufficient cities presented in this category can be defined in terms of the way they relate to 'their' territory, understood as a set of resources.

The possible responses can be summed up in two mutually exclusive general approaches which nonetheless represent the two sides of the same coin. On one side is the idea of returning to a model 'after nature', which would maximize the relationship with the territory, and on the other side is the model of the enclosed autonomous city, which would minimize that relationship. The 'after nature' approach to the city is essentially a matter of going back to neo-rural or pre-industrial models, and applying these to the contemporary city, or to parts of the present-day city or its annihilated remains. These strategies seek to restore a balance to the relationship with the territory, opting for lower levels of comfort, consuming only what is produced, utilizing renewable resources and reducing the environmental impact to the minimum. This was the model of most ancient civilizations, but it is also the same type of development as that of the individual living being in the natural state, perfectly inserted in the biological cycle of nature.

In contrast, the second approach could take the form of an almost completely autonomous infrastructure essentially independent of the territory. We can imagine mobile or hypercompact cities capable of being dismantled or expanded: plug-in cities that call to mind space ships or ocean liners, as in the visionary experiments of the nineteen sixties. In many cases this model reinterprets and takes its extreme consequences the concept of self-sufficiency of an apartment block: vertical cities, floating cuboids virtually indifferent to the environment around them. We are a step away from no longer needing the planet Earth.

LIVING LANDSCAPES

URBAN GREEN

BIO INFRASTRUCTURES

ENERGY SYSTEMS

PARAMETRIC URBANISM

SOCIAL & COLLABORATIVE

THEORIES & STRATEGIES

FINALIST

SYMBIOTIC LANDSCAPE

Luz Mireia
Alejandro Mui

mireia.luzarraga@gmail.com

Spain

Cities on the XX century have become closed entities unable to recycle their inner processes. For our time we would like to purpose cities that would invert this dynamics turning into an artificial ecosystem based on the exchange of energy. Through the injection of feedback cycle systems on the city, it's waste can become the base of new complex forms of living, coherents with the environment's possibilities.

The project is no longer more than a re-energizing system which builds a new symbiotic landscape, through accumulation, transformation and dissipation of energy coherent with the city. A plantation of objects which gets profit of the strongs winds of the coast, provides the cities with pure water, through the purification of waste water generated by them, and desalination of sea water, as well as completing the public space. The towers mainly work in two directions. On one hand they generate and recycle the water that supplies the cities avoiding pollutions. On the other hand they are in charge of re-activating the public space which is becoming smaller nowadays, that we ignore its possibilities of uniting the society. The project is made out of small ecosystems related to the purification process, which generate a new kind of green spaces for the city.

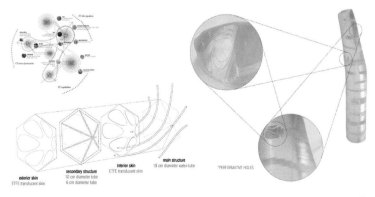

exterior skin
ETFE translucent skin

secondary structure
10 cm diameter tube
6 cm diameter tube

interior skin
ETFE translucent skin

main structure
18 cm diameter water-tube

*PERFORMATIVE HOLES

The group of buildings works as a big organism which exchanges energy with its surroundings. The tower's big holes let the wind pass through generating the necessary eolic energy for to complete the water-purification cycle. The water accumulated in tanks in the surroundings of the towers, goes up to the top in order to descend slowly by gravity passing through purification plant systems, creating vertical gardens. The public programme of the tower gets profit of these gardens to generate artificial atmospheres through intensificating processes.

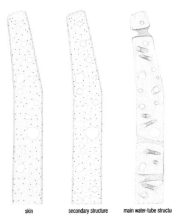

skin   secondary structure   main water-tube structure

LIVING LANDSCAPES

URBAN GREEN

BIO INFRASTRUCTURES

ENERGY SYSTEMS

PARAMETRIC URBANISM

SOCIAL & COLLABORATIVE

THEORIES & STRATEGIES

LIVING LANDSCAPES

URBAN GREEN

BIO INFRASTRUCTURES

ENERGY SYSTEMS

PARAMETRIC URBANISM

SOCIAL & COLLABORATIVE

THEORIES & STRATEGIES

ARCHITECTURE AS INFRASTRUCTURE

Di Oronzo Antonio
Masashi Kobayashi
Khan Shibly
Oriana Lustgarten

ado@bluarch.com

United States

Residential Sky-scraper in New York City

This residential tower is a hybrid. It offers pods for transient residential units and/or produces energy when/where these units are not present. Three super-columns act as cores and as structural system. Pods are piled on and around each super-column and host residential units, or wind mills, or solar panels. Every 5-to-7 stories larger, green pods span all three super-columns to brace them in a truss-like system. Nine large-size wind mills top the tower and blur in the wind…

This model of inhabitation finds scale significance if repeated and scattered in a fractal distribution in urban settings across the globe. The residential units would move from tower to tower, along with its inhabitants in a highly entropic narrative. As it produces energy, this building is energy self-reliant and a contributing node to the electric grid. Therefore, this tower has a negative CO2 footprint, and transcends its architectural identity by acting as infrastructure.

An urban framework where architecture is also infrastructure produces a shift in the balance of real estate values and safe-guards the overall economical stability of a large-scale ecological project. In fact, this model of infrastructural architecture would entail the participation of public funds, and/or the collaboration of private and public resources and figures. Thus far, only a change in policy has been able to create the economical viability for environmentally feasible architecture. This hybrid model which overlays architecture and infrastructure further establishes the importance of a new sustainable paradigm.

Further, mass-customizable residential units can be fabricated and installed to suit specific needs. This approach opens up traditional construction methods to new design/build processes where design and installation are purely based on form and performance. New social models are forming, and fluidity of relationships and mobility of the smallest social units are pushing for a more ductile economical model for the construction industry. Hence, mass-customization is a natural, viable and necessary consequence. These premises offer scenarios of an ever-changing architecture in a continually varying urban setting. They portend a shift in the conception of portable residence and architecture without site. In this conceptual framework the diagrammatic approach of modern times has no longer relevance.

PROPOSED NEW
SOUTH STREET SEAPORT
NEW YORK CITY, NY   USA

NEW RESIDENTIAL TOWER

LIVING LANDSCAPES

URBAN GREEN

BIO INFRASTRUCTURES

ENERGY SYSTEMS

PARAMETRIC URBANISM

SOCIAL & COLLABORATIVE

THEORIES & STRATEGIES

LIVING LANDSCAPES

URBAN GREEN

BIO INFRASTRUCTURES

ENERGY SYSTEMS

PARAMETRIC URBANISM

SOCIAL & CO LABORATIVE

THEORIES & STRATEGIES

SUBMERGIA

 FINALIST

Wit Andrew
Thaddeus Jusczyk
andrewjohnwit@gmail.com

United States

Littered with suburban communities built on reclaimed land, San Francisco Bay is only one example of a global city to be effected by sea level rise. With these low-lying areas to soon be repossessed by the waters, residents will be forced to look for alternative ways of living. Rather than viewing the impending deluge as a tragedy, could it instead be an opportunity? Rather than taking drastic steps to mitigate the potential flooding, cant we simply let theses cities return to the water? Rather than transplanting the displaced suburbanites to a new sprawling community, cant we find a new alternative that minimizes the impact on the land and water?

Submergea, an off-the-grid, low impact community for living and working, provides a new network for urban growth.

Hasn't the suburban dream outlived its potential?

Foster City

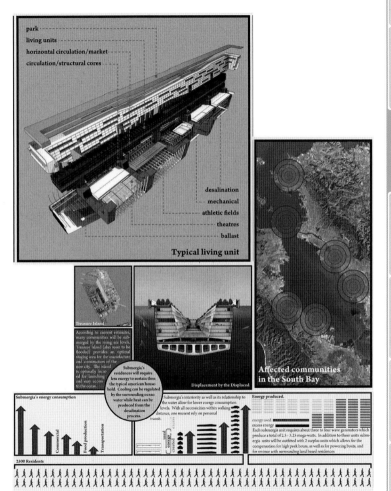

park
living units
horizontal circulation/market
circulation/structural cores

desalination
mechanical
athletic fields
theatres
ballast

Typical living unit

Treasure Island

According to current estimates, many communities will be submerged by the rising sea levels. Treasure Island (also soon to be flooded) provides an optimal staging area for the manufacture and construction of the new city. The island is optimally located for launching and easy access to the ocean.

Submergia's residences will require less energy to sustain then the typical american household. Cooling can be regulated by the surrounding ocean water while heat can be produced from the desalination process.

Displacement by the Displaced

Affected communities in the South Bay

Submergia's energy consumption

Commercial
Food production
Transportation

2500 Residents

Submergia's interiority as well as its relationship to the water allow for lower energy consumption levels. With all necessities within walking distance, one musent rely on personal transit.

energy used
energy created

Energy produced.

energy used
excess energy
Each submergia unit requires about three to four wave generators which produce a total of 2.5 - 3.25 mega-watts. In addition to these units submergia units will be outfitted with 2 surplus units which allows for the compensation for high peek hours, as well as for powering boats, and for revenue with surrounding land based residences

LIVING LANDSCAPES

URBAN GREEN

BIO INFRASTRUCTURES

ENERGY SYSTEMS

PARAMETRIC URBANISM

SOCIAL & COLLABORATIVE

THEORIES & STRATEGIES

Submergia's procession from Treasure Island, through the Golden Gate, provides the bay area with an exciting spectacle to remember.

164

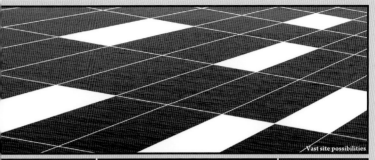
Vast site possibilities

Visitors arrive by boat at the park level, which is filled with trees, jogging and cycling paths, and places to lounge. Descending from the park, they then move through the residential layers, which are bisected by the horizontal circulation/market level. Below, they find the large open expanse of lawn, outdoor theatres, athletic facilities, with offices, theatres, and community spaces underneath.

More than a bedroom community, Submergia offers all the benefits of an urban lifestyle. Schools, parks, restaurants, bars, shopping, theatres, offices, athletic fields, swimming pools, and community spaces are all within short walking distances. San Francisco and other communities are only a short ferry ride away, allowing for all the mobility without the noise and hastle of daily traffic.

"Sure beats the old office."

LIVING LANDSCAPES

URBAN GREEN

BIO INFRASTRUCTURES

ENERGY SYSTEMS

PARAMETRIC URBANISM

SOCIAL & COLLABORATIVE

THEORIES & STRATEGIES

LIVING LANDSCAPES

URBAN GREEN

BIO INFRASTRUCTURES

ENERGY SYSTEMS

PARAMETRIC URBANISM

SOCIAL & COLLABORATIVE

THEORIES & STRATEGIES

METEORITE BEIJING 2080

Dong Tao
Jingyun Ye
Zhihai Ma
Na Lin
Meizi Xiao

fa_china@126.com

China

Beijing is an ancient city with three thousand years of being founded and eight hundred years of being as a capital. In this city, Hutong(alley) and Siheyuan (quadrangle) are the representatives of its history of architecture. In modern era, resulting from the endless demolition of Hutong and Siheyuan, Beijing, this old city, is over the hill.

Our research purposes focus on the coexistence of the new and old urban zones, which can remain the scene of the ancient buildings and also enhance the inhabitants' living quality, namely balancing the ancient buildings and the urban development.

Due to the formation and spreading from the points to the areas and the whole network system of "meteorite" step by step, Beijing will finally hold the new self-sufficient survival system.
The self-sufficient "meteorite" system can obtain the energy from the air, sunshine and wastes, and then it will deal with the transformation to support the self-supply, repairing and development. In view of the actuality as crowded public space and rare virescence area in Hutongs, its interior space will be divided into the community center and greenhouse. The central closed structure will contain the mini garden.

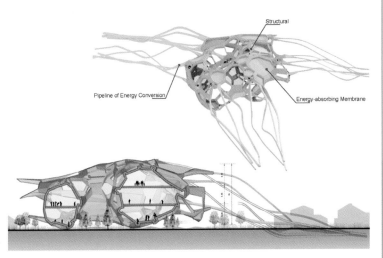

Structural

Pipeline of Energy Conversion

Energy-absorbing Membrane

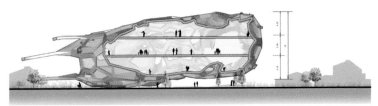

LIVING LANDSCAPES

URBAN GREEN

BIO INFRASTRUCTURES

ENERGY SYSTEMS

PARAMETRIC URBANISM

SOCIAL & COLLABORATIVE

THEORIES & STRATEGIES

LIVING LANDSCAPES

URBAN GREEN

BIO INFRASTRUCTURES

ENERGY SYSTEMS

PARAMETRIC URBANISM

SOCIAL & COLLABORATIVE

THEORIES & STRATEGIES

SOAK CITY

FINALIST

Peter Cook
Gavin Robotham
Lorene Raure
Maria Knutsson-Hall

info@crabstudio.net

United Kingdom

The project looks at the effect of global-warmth flooding upon an existing urbanized area, London, within the 21st century. It suggests that remnants of substantial structures might survive – with their lower levels flooded.

It suggests that connection routes can be reestablished at higher levels and that a tougher attitude towards the use of marginal land for vegetable growing be adopted. Terracing and dangling growth-zones wherever possible.

The new built form concentrates upon the setting-up of a primary ring of shelter, with a loose geometry that establishes the structure. This is made up of a variety of components : recycled strips of old steelwork, timbers from roofs, rescued elements from the oncoming floods. A similar eclecticism applies to the outer skin : so that these 'shelter cones' are concentrating upon one aim : the maximum shelter for the minimum new material.

The dwellings then 'hang' inside, using the ring as basic support structure. The resulting 'building' is then ready to be colonized by planting : vegetable husbandry instead of traditional 'architectural' façade. Thus the built form is a hybrid between vertical allotment, 'castle', windshield and tower of optimism.

LIVING LANDSCAPES

URBAN GREEN

BIO INFRASTRUCTURES

ENERGY SYSTEMS

PARAMETRIC URBANISM

SOCIAL & COLLABORATIVE

THEORIES & STRATEGIES

LIVING LANDSCAPES

URBAN GREEN

BIO-INFRASTRUCTURES

ENERGY SYSTEMS

PARAMETRIC URBANISM

SOCIAL & COLLABORATIVE

THEORIES & STRATEGIES

WATER FUEL
THE PLAN FOR A SELF-
SUSTAINING NEW YORK

Rychiee Espinosa
Seth McDowell

rychiee@gmail.com

United States

For the last 10 years hundreds of engineers, inventors, and scientists have been investigating the possibility of using water for fuel by means of electrolysis. It was not until recently when John Kanzius, a retired engineer, discovered an efficient method of burning saltwater with radio frequencies that commercial interests in the method began to rise. This prospect of running one's car on water stimulates a plethora of questions about economy, distribution, dependence, and the commoditization of the natural resource. A new transportation network which depends on this new fueling system gathers the energy required for electrolysis through the use energy-harvesting mats, situated on the edge of the island on the water. The location and proximity of these mats to other means of transportation allows for an easier East-West commute across New York City. Thus, a more efficient commute is created and the air is kept clean as the exhaust created by water fuel is simply water itself. As a result,

ENERGY-GENERATION AND RECREATION COMBINE TO FORM A NEW LANDSCAPE.

Each unit within the fueling mat contains an electrolyzer which requires power collected by wave energy-harvesting components. In turn, these electrolyzers are then capable of generating fire and heat from water extracted from the river. A sectional perspective describes this system as a heated beach, which extends its seasonal use beyond the summertime into the winter.

On the water, a new type of public space is rendered: the images of the fueling mat illustrate a type of environment that emerges from this new transportation network.

Also reliant on fuel, are secondary spaces which contain barbeque pits and heated baths as a means to generate further personal connections with the water-hydrogen technology. Emerging from the infrastructural demands for fuel is a new recreational landscape for Manhattan.

LIVING LANDSCAPES

URBAN GREEN

BIO INFRASTRUCTURES

ENERGY SYSTEMS

PARAMETRIC URBANISM

SOCIAL & COLLABORATIVE

THEORIES & STRATEGIES

RELAX ON A HEATED BEACH OF BUBBLES INFRASTRUCTURE BECOMES RECREATIONAL

Each unit within the fueling mat contains an electrolyzer which requires power collected by wave energy-harvesting components. In turn, these electrolyzers are then capable of generating fire and heat from water extracted from the river. A sectional perspective describes this system as a heated beach, which extends its seasonal use beyond the summertime into the winter.

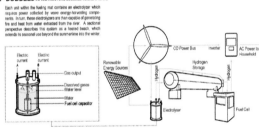

ONE ELECTROLYZER
THE PROCESS OF EXTRACTING HYDROGEN FROM WATER

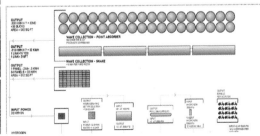

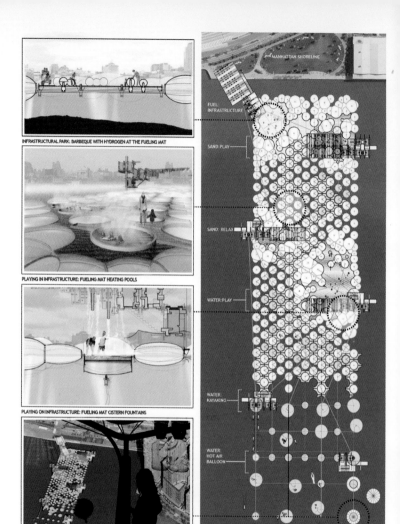

INFRASTRUCTURAL PARK: BARBEQUE WITH HYDROGEN AT THE FUELING MAT

PLAYING IN INFRASTRUCTURE: FUELING MAT HEATING POOLS

PLAYING ON INFRASTRUCTURE: FUELING MAT CISTERN FOUNTAINS

ADDED RECREATIONAL VALUE: VIEW FROM A HOT AIR BALLOON RIDE

MANHATTAN SHORELINE

FUEL:
INFRASTRUCTURE

SAND: PLAY

SAND: RELAX

WATER: PLAY

WATER:
KAYAKING

WATER:
HOT AIR
BALLOON

LIVING LANDSCAPES

URBAN GREEN

BIO INFRASTRUCTURES

ENERGY SYSTEMS

PARAMETRIC URBANISM

SOCIAL & COLLABORATIVE

THEORIES & STRATEGIES

THE RIVER BECOMES A PUBLIC SPACE INFRASTRUCTURE CREATES A NEW LANDSCAPE

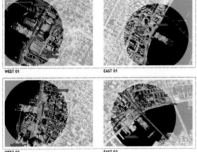

WEST 01

EAST 01

WEST 02

EAST 02

EAST-WEST CONNECTIONS BASED ON THE 2000' RADIUS OF COMFORTABLE WALKING DISTANCE

For the last 10 years hundreds of engineers, inventors, and scientists have been investigating the possibility of using water for fuel by means of electrolysis. It was not until recently when John Kanzius, a retired engineer, discovered an efficient method of burning saltwater with radio frequencies that commercial interests in the method began to rise. The prospect of running one's car on water stimulates a plethora of questions about economy, distribution, dependance, and the commodization of the natural resource.

A new transportation network which depends on this new fueling system gathers the energy required for electrolysis through the use energy-harvesting mats, situated on the edge of the island on the water. The location and proximity of these mats to other means of transportation allows for an easier East-West commute across New York City. Thus, a more efficient commute is created and the air is kept clean as the exhaust created by water fuel is simply water itself. As a result, ENERGY-GENERATION AND RECREATION COMBINE TO FORM A NEW LANDSCAPE.

UNITS SERVING MANHATTAN **365**
2002 455 SQ. FT OF MAT

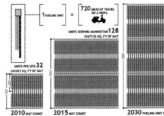

$\begin{bmatrix} 1 \text{ FUELING UNIT} \end{bmatrix} = \begin{bmatrix} 720 \text{ MILES OF TRAVEL ON A VESPA} \end{bmatrix}$

UNITS SERVING MANHATTAN **128**
1047132 SQ. FT OF MAT

UNITS PER SITE **32**
261021 SQ. FT OF MAT

WATER FUEL
THE PLAN FOR A SELF-SUSTAINING NEW YORK CITY

2010 MAT COUNT   2015 MAT COUNT   2030 FUELING UNIT COUNT

MULTIPLICITY AND SCALE OF MANHATTAN FUELING MATS

ECOTOPIA

Jiang Bin

archinanju@hotmail.com

China

Nowadays, the ecosystem is suffering serious damages. My proposal is to insert a new restoration system in the interior of the city where the living environment is deteriorating, in an attempt to accelerate the system's recycling and regeneration with the help of eco-technologies so as to restore the unbalanced ecosystem. Restructure of society frame : post-physiocracy transplanting countrysides in the city

The eco-community alters the former concepts of community, unifying the traditionally separated communities and promoting the trans-community exchanges. In addition, insertion of the eco-agriculture into the city will result in a new social type "Urban farmer".

Formulas of the system restoration of the urban ecosystem

• Architect = Organizer of the production
• Architecture + Eco-technique = Eco-machine
• (Eco-machine + Bio-agriculture + Urban peasant) x n = Eco-tribe
• Eco-tribe + Community exist = Eco-community
• Eco-community x n + Eco-system = Eco-city

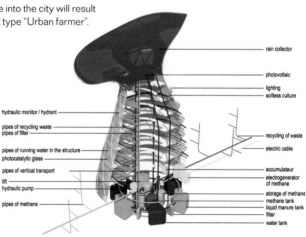

rain collector

photovoltaic

lighting
soilless culture

hydraulic monitor / hydrant

pipes of recycling waste
pipes of filter

recycling of waste

pipes of running water in the structure
photocatalytic glass

electric cable

pipes of vertical transport

accumulateur
electrogenerator of methane

lift
hydraulic pump

storage of methane
methane tank

pipes of methane

liquid manure tank
filter
water tank

LIVING LANDSCAPES

URBAN GREEN

BIO INFRASTRUCTURES

ENERGY SYSTEMS

PARAMETRIC URBANISM

SOCIAL & COLLABORATIVE

THEORIES & STRATEGIES

THE CONCEPTUAL DECISION OF THE BUILDING OF THE SELF-REGULATING BUILDING

Filimonov Vadym

ar.vadim@mail.ru

Ukraine

The ecology problem is one of global problems of the present. Feature of this problem consists that it has universal character, that is infringes on interests of all nations of the world, threatens with destruction to all mankind, it requires effective decisions, demands joint efforts of the states and the people.

Society development was always accompanied by destructive influence on the nature. Constant development of the industry, transport and agriculture and so on demands sharp increase in expenses of energy and attracts behind itself escalating loading on the nature. Now as a result of intensive human activity there is even a climate change. Clearly, that these changes will put the huge problems connected with housekeeping, reproduction of necessary conditions of their life before people.

Economic activities of the person already attract presently behind itself climate change, it influences a chemical compound of water and air pools of the Earth, on animal and planet flora, on weigh its shape.

LIVING LANDSCAPES

URBAN GREEN

BIO INFRASTRUCTURES

ENERGY SYSTEMS

PARAMETRIC URBANISM

SOCIAL & COLLABORATIVE

THEORIES & STRATEGIES

Main principles of a self-regulating building

1 — automatic creations of comfort of
people living in a building

2 — protection of inhabitants of a complex against negative influences of the
atmospheric phenomena (an excessive
radio-activity of the sun, a wind)

3 — maximum accumulation, transformation and careful use of resources (a solar
energy, inflow-outflow, fluctuations of
level of world ocean, heating, ventilation,
accumulation and storage of quantity
of energy of a complex necessary for
functioning)

4 — device of the developed infrastructure:
parkings, restaurants, business complexes.
The improving and sports centres.
Complex functioning on independently
saved up resources

5 — Main principle of a complex

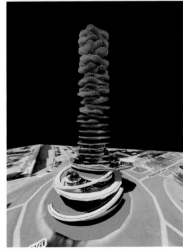

LIVING LANDSCAPES

URBAN GREEN

BIO INFRASTRUCTURES

ENERGY SYSTEMS

PARAMETRIC URBANISM

SOCIAL & COLLABORATIVE

THEORIES & STRATEGIES

MEGA CITY BLOCK

Kyaw Aung

athukyaw@gmail.com

Myanmar

Architects and city planners have long agreed upon the higher eco-friendliness of urban life than that of suburban sprawl. In this "Mega City Block" design proposal, the urban grid idea is reexamined and retrofitted into a highly sustainable agricultural-industrial-urban complex. Everything that a city life can offer _ government offices, residential units, entertainments, street life, hotels, park, recreation centers, and etc _ is contained in each mega city block. The city is designed as a car-free zone, connected by an underground light-rail system. Every single building in the mega block is linked by the elevated urban streets where residents can walk around or jog or buy at the grocery stores or just enjoy the aerial view of the surrounding agricultural fields. Around the mega city block, wind turbines are placed to generate electricity, and every roof top of the uniform high buildings, which would be difficult to obtain in a typical city, is equipped with solar firms. Rain water is also collected from every rooftop for grey water recycling. So, the intention is to create a highly sustainable, carbon-neutral, mega city block through collectiveness while enriching the lives of city dwelling.

Architects and city planners have long agreed upon the higher ecofriendliness of urban life than that of suburban sprawl. In this "Mega City Block" design proposal, the urban grid idea is reexamined and retrofitted into a highly sustainable agricultural-industrial-urban complex.

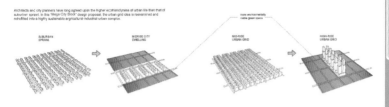

LIVING LANDSCAPES

URBAN GREEN

BIO INFRASTRUCTURES

ENERGY SYSTEMS

PARAMETRIC URBANISM

SOCIAL & COLLABORATIVE

THEORIES & STRATEGIES

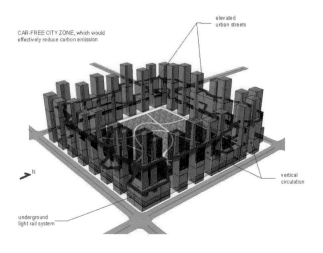

CAR-FREE CITY ZONE, which would
effectively reduce carbon emission

elevated
urban streets

vertical
circulation

underground
light rail system

N

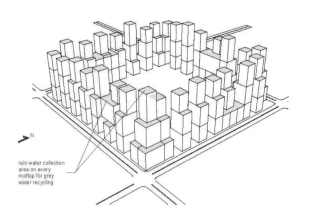

rain water collection
area on every
rooftop for grey
water recycling

N

LIVING LANDSCAPES

URBAN GREEN

BIO INFRASTRUCTURES

ENERGY SYSTEMS

PARAMETRIC URBANISM

SOCIAL & COLLABORATIVE

THEORIES & STRATEGIES

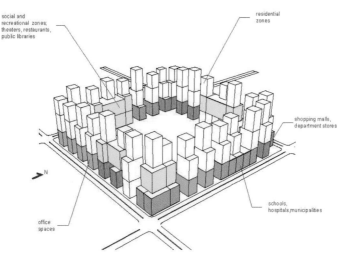

social and
recreational zones;
theaters, restaurants,
public libraries

residential
zones

shopping malls,
department stores

schools,
hospitals, municipalities

office
spaces

N

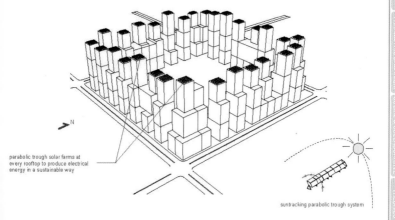

parabolic trough solar farms at
every rooftop to produce electrical
energy in a sustainable way

N

suntracking parabolic trough system

FILTER TOWER
THE SELF SUFFICIENT
BUILDING

Contreras Daniel - UEES

dimitry_maximi@hotmail.com

Ecuador

The objective of this project is to make recycling of existing cities looking for a way to correct the mistakes that have caused irreparable harm not only to individuals but also to the environment. After analysis it was determined that one of the major problems facing large cities today is the lack of safety due to the precarious and outdated water distribution systems. Another error is the creation of large dams for generating electricity, through blockade of the rivers, damaging every living thing that uses it, seriously affecting the environment resulting in altering the course of nature.

With these parameters the idea is to create "FILTER TOWERS" which are buildings with implemented water treatment system for a more efficient and safe suppliy of drinking water.

The process consists in prosecuting the water from a river or lake into the building through a canal or pipeline 0.00 on the surface, then get down on the facade in a cascade and with the force of the fall turbines operate generating electricity for the building. As the water falls, it is filtered through purifing water filters.

This project is about giving a new perspective to the design of water dams, in which both the potable water system and electricity system are complementary.

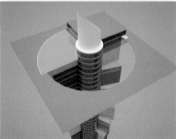

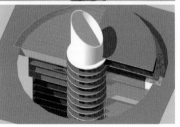

LIVING LANDSCAPES

URBAN GREEN

BIO INFRASTRUCTURES

ENERGY SYSTEMS

PARAMETRIC URBANISM

SOCIAL & ECO LABORATIVE

THEORIES & STRATEGIES

MADRID 20XX

Iglesias Javier

javi31x84@hotmail.com

Spain

The city will not spread any more...new developments will occupy the space already constructed.

Proposed strategy
— Backpack
— Cover
— Cantilever

A model of city is proposed in which the city expansion occurs in the space already built, to prevent from depletion of the territory.

The proposal is based on using existing buildings as "artificial territory" for new buildings.

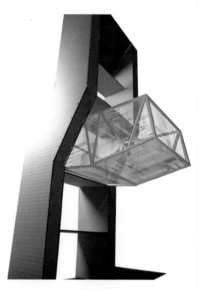

The project is located in the existing parking space next to the Santiago Bernabeu. We propose a large green photovoltaic blanket that wraps the new building that climbs over the facade of the stadium where are situated the hotel rooms. The public spaces of the hotel are situated in the ground level of the street, while the private spaces of hotel rooms are located in the capsules hung on structure of the stadium. Access to the capsules of the rooms is done by circulation tubes that connect the lifts with the rest of the areas. Thus both functions, hotel and football stadium may have independent uses. The number of capsules room might be extended, depending on seasonal demand, or due to major events.

The skin of the building is a major source of solar energy through photovoltaic panels that generate electricity. Besides the façade allows to clean out the water generated in the use of the building through Phytodepuration tubes that form a closed loop along the entire facade. The capsules are built at street level, to be moved later to the proposed site. This saves time and auxiliary materials in construction.

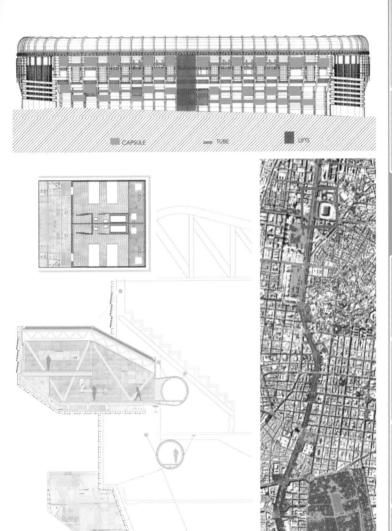

CAPSULE   TUBE   LIFTS

LIVING LANDSCAPES

URBAN GREEN

BIO-INFRASTRUCTURES

ENERGY SYSTEMS

PARAMETRIC URBANISM

SOCIAL & COLLABORATIVE

THEORIES & STRATEGIES

2009

2012

2016

LIVING LANDSCAPES

URBAN GREEN

BIO INFRASTRUCTURES

ENERGY SYSTEMS

PARAMETRIC URBANISM

SOCIAL & COLLABORATIVE

THEORIES & STRATEGIES

CAPSULE HOUSING

Domingo Ballestin Javier
Juan Madrigueras

javidomingo_82@hotmail.com

Spain

With the aim of promoting discussion and research about the hypothetical future habitat, this proposal borns to be a vision of a XXI th century city. Considering on the social characteristics, values and lifestyles of contemporary society and its impact on the future.

Thus arises this project as an experiment or self-criticism, in a context in which social ideals of globalization, universality, equality, capitalism, communication, dispersion ... have been taken to an extreme, one initial theoretical assumption, not so distant from our present.

Taking into account as a significant event of nowadays in which virtual worlds and interest of contemporary society to be always informed (on-line), is common to all individuals. The idea is to produce a core-person housing capable of being transported and connected to a universal terminal, which will provide all the necessities for the development of life and productive activity of the individual.

These terminals or nodes will be able to group together in order to form new and self-sufficient towns.

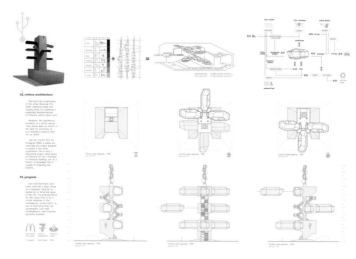

LIVING LANDSCAPES

URBAN GREEN

BIO INFRASTRUCTURES

ENERGY SYSTEMS

PARAMETRIC URBANISM

SOCIAL & COLLABORATIVE

THEORIES & STRATEGIES

01 Telecommunications transmitter/receiver
02 Internet transmitter/receiver
03 GPS transmitter/receiver
04 New technologies transmitter/receiver
05 Telecommunications pole
06 Telecommunications pole base/adapter
07 Collector/collector water deposit
08 Connectable habitation module
09 Photovoltaic panels
10 Node connection modules
11 Communication stairs/viewpoint
12 Sewer node
13 Base/equipment connecting
14 Landscaped equipments
15 Groundwater closed circuit of temperature comfort system

CANARY WHARF + POPLAR - LONDON 2015

Edwards John

john.edwards@network.rca.ac.uk

United Kingdom

Self Sufficiency depends on Sustainability. Sustainability depends on diversity. Diversity depends on understanding. The Learning City is the Self Sufficient City. The Self Sufficient city understands: The city is composed of destinations that are programmatically and not geographically determined; and the journeys between them.

It is composed of a discontinuous archipelago of post-urban fragments. Fragmentation has led to ghettoisation and severe inequality.

Sustainability depends on diversity, interaction and inclusion.

Sustainability depends on learning, and applied understanding.

A stitching process is required Canary Wharf + Poplar

Two fragments of the post-urban condition, neighbouring but separated by a major transport artery, Canary Wharf and Poplar offer contrasting visions of contemporary London.

Whilst Canary Wharf became swollen with the excess of high capitalism, Poplar was left to ruin - with some of the highest levels of living deprivation in Europe.

Now both wallow in the mire of the post-Crunch economy.

No city can be truly Self Sufficient with such a schism. The North Quays, Aspen Way, Poplar DLR and Poplar High Street become the testbed for the new urban patchwork.

Self Sufficiency depends upon optimising what is already there.

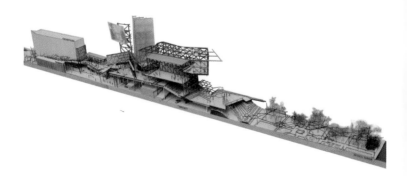

LIVING LANDSCAPES

URBAN GREEN

BIO INFRASTRUCTURES

ENERGY SYSTEMS

PARAMETRIC URBANISM

SOCIAL & COLLABORATIVE

THEORIES & STRATEGIES

LIVING LANDSCAPES

URBAN GREEN

BIO INFRASTRUCTURES

ENERGY SYSTEMS

PARAMETRIC URBANISM

SOCIAL & COLLABORATIVE

THEORIES & STRATEGIES

ONE CUBIC KILO-METER CITY

Marc Ordureau

marcordureau@hotmail.com

France

The self-sufficiency concept for a city induces two fundamental steps. First minimizing its energy, water and raw materials consumption and reducing its waste production. Then making the production systems (energy, food, ...) more efficient to reach this autonomy. 1km3 is a theoretical model of extremely dense urban development.

It is a city of one cubic kilometer (1km x 1km x 1km) able to accommodate approximately 1 million inhabitants.1 km is a measurement unit that captures both the urban scale (e.g. the density of a city is measured in inhabitants per km2) and the human scale (a person needs 15 minutes to walk 1km far).

Brussels = 1 million of inhabitants = 30 510 km2

1KM3 = 1 million of inhabitants = 1 km2

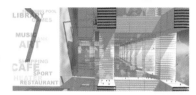

1 — Saving land.

The saved ground can be used to develop local agriculture and natural parks, easily accessible by the residents of 1km3. 1km3 supports the development of food self-sufficiency and the protection of sensitive natural areas (e.g. aquatic ecosystems such as swamps, rivers...).

2 — A more compact city consuming less energy and matter.

The extreme compactness of 1km3 limits the travel distances.

The horizontal journeys are done by foot (15 minutes across town). The vertical journeys are done by high speed elevators that give access to the different levels as a "vertical subway". 1km3 gets its supplies through a system of overhead networks (water, electricity, gas...) easier to maintain or renew than a system of underground networks, therefore optimizing it to avoid leaks, losses and obsolescence.

3 — An evolving city.

1km3's peripheral structure is essentially dedicated to housing and shops. This structure consists in platforms suitable for free arrangement and can therefore evolve for demographic or lifestyle means. This flexibility ensures a city in constant renewal.

Surfaces and voids of 1km3 host renewable energy systems (wind, solar panels...) as part of the global energy supply.

4 — Reconciling urban with human.

1km3 has a strong visual identity, becoming an icon and giving the inhabitants a strong sense of belonging and a strong cultural identity. This city is not made of buildings and monuments. 1km3 is both a building and a monument.

It combines the idea of a functional building and a symbol.

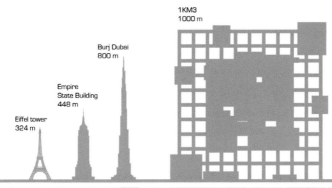

Eiffel tower
324 m

Empire
State Building
448 m

Burj Dubai
800 m

1KM3
1000 m

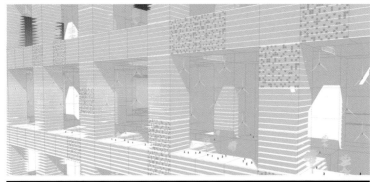

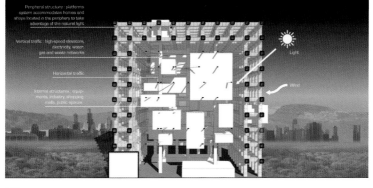

Peripheral structure : platforms
system accommodates homes and
shops located in the periphery to take
advantage of the natural light.

Vertical traffic: high-speed elevators,
electricity, water,
gas and waste networks

Horizontal traffic

Internal structures : equipments, industry, shopping
malls, public spaces

Light

Wind

LIVING LANDSCAPES

URBAN GREEN

BIO INFRASTRUCTURES

ENERGY SYSTEMS

PARAMETRIC URBANISM

SOCIAL & COLLABORATIVE

THEORIES & STRATEGIES

LIVING LANDSCAPES

URBAN GREEN

BIO INFRASTRUCTURES

ENERGY SYSTEMS

PARAMETRIC URBANISM

SOCIAL & COLLABORATIVE

THEORIES & STRATEGIES

21ST CENTURY CITY - AN URBAN FUTURE

Till Groner

till.groner@gmail.com

Germany

The supply- rise is a city-centralization-tool, that canalizes neighborhoods and embraces all infrastructures for future sky communities, which benefit from urban proximity and equal income generating possibilities in fast growing cities of especially newly industrializing countries. Prospectively buildings can be planned as "easy-extension-able" because supply and access could be provided external and central.

The facilitation of building-upgrades would reduce destruction and ensure the conservation of social and cultural goods.

Combined with a net of permanent secondary public transportation, the "suppligh-rises" as foyers of whole neighborhoods could simplify regional traffic and obviate the need for individual vehicles.

Central building supply would rise the efficiency of any water treatment, garbage recycling and power buffering from low intensive regenerative resources.

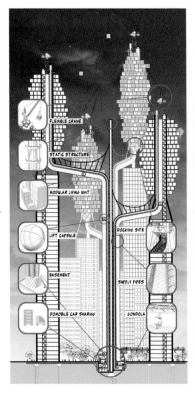

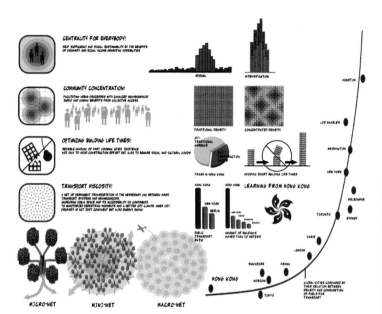

CENTRALITY FOR EVERYBODY!
SELF SUFFICIENCY AND SOCIAL SUSTAINABILITY IN THE BENEFITS
OF PROXIMITY AND EQUAL INCOME-GENERATING POSSIBILITIES

COMMUNITY CONCENTRATION!
FACILITATING URBAN PROCESSES WITH ENHANCED NEIGHBOURHOOD
SUPPLY AND SHARING BENEFITS FROM COLLECTIVE ACCESS

OPTIMIZING BUILDING LIFE TIMES!
SENSIBLE HANDLING OF FAST GROWING CITIES' EXISTENCE
NOT ONLY TO AVOID CONSTRUCTION EFFORT BUT ALSO TO BEWARE SOCIAL AND CULTURAL GOODS

TRANSPORT VISCOSITY!
A NET OF PERMANENT TRANSPORTATION IS THE NECESSARY LINK BETWEEN MASS
TRANSPORT SYSTEMS AND NEIGHBOURHOODS
INCREASING PUBLIC SPACE AND ITS ACCESSIBILITY DO CONTRIBUTE
TO UNMOTORIZED PEDESTRIAN MOVEMENTS AND A BETTER CITY CLIMATE INNER CITY
PROXIMITY IS NOT JUST CONVENIENT BUT ALSO ENERGY SAVING

SPRAWL   INTENSIFICATION

TRADITIONAL DENSITY   CONCENTRATED DENSITY

TRASH IN HONG KONG   AVOIDING SHORT BUILDING LIFE TIMES

LEARNING FROM HONG KONG

PUBLIC TRANSPORT RATIO   AMOUNT OF BUILDINGS HIGHER THAN 50 METERS

HONG KONG

HOUSTON
LOS ANGELES
WASHINGTON
NEW YORK
MELBOURNE
TORONTO
SYDNEY
PARIS
LONDON
SINGAPORE   VIENNA
MOSCOW
TOKYO

GLOBAL CITIES COMPARED BY
THEIR RELATION BETWEEN
DENSITY AND CONSUMPTION
OF FUELS FOR
TRANSPORT

MICRO-NET   MINI-NET   MACRO-NET

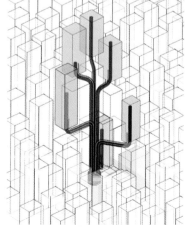

LIVING LANDSCAPES

URBAN GREEN

BIO INFRASTRUCTURES

ENERGY SYSTEMS

PARAMETRIC URBANISM

SOCIAL & COLLABORATIVE

THEORIES & STRATEGIES

LIVING LANDSCAPES

URBAN GREEN

BIO INFRASTRUCTURES

ENERGY SYSTEMS

PARAMETRIC URBANISM

SOCIAL & COLLABORATIVE

THEORIES & STRATEGIES

ENERGY
SYSTEMS

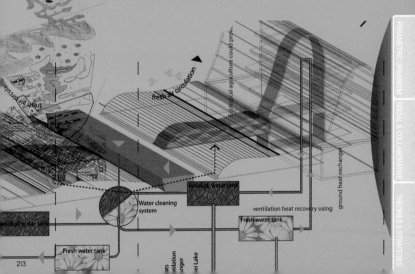

LIVING LANDSCAPES

URBAN GREEN

BIO-INFRASTRUCTURES

ENERGY SYSTEMS

PARAMETRIC URBANISM

SOCIAL & COLLABORATIVE

THEORIES & STRATEGIES

fresh air circulation

ecological agriculture could prov..

fresh air circulation

Water cleaning
system

Residual water tank

ground heat exchanger

ventilation heat recovery using

Fresh water tank

esidual water tank

Fresh water tank

Fresh water tank

el Lake

ats

tilation

nger

ENERGY SYSTEMS

Territory can be understood as a set of overlapping networks — infrastructural networks that determine the use, the capacity, the impact and other qualities of urban space. These networks should not be seen as independent entities but rather as moderators of interwoven conditions that, by establishing different balances between themselves, increase the potentiality of 'things' happening. As such, they are the object of design strategies, regarded from a wider viewpoint. The projects in this category are concerned with integrating energy flow networks into the design proposals. The issues addressed range from poverty and natural resources to the quality of urban spaces and the impact of tourism. It is important to take note of the social extensions of any project on the urban scale and its implementation through environmental strategies. The city is seen as a dynamic infrastructural grid which redefines the boundary between the public and the private, the individual and the collective, the artificial and the natural, the virtual and the physical.

Energy cycles, as a multiscalar concept rather than a finite autonomous system, contribute to the design of sustainable development. Functional interactions between the habitat and its environment are made possible because of the network of infrastructures, so the need for multiscalarity arises in energy networks, too, because whatever the scale of the intervention it is interconnected with the world. The way energy networks are deployed configures the impact or footprint that different actions have on their immediate or more extended environment.

Recent history has been constructed on the basis of centralized systems of energy, information or production. The approach taken by contemporary design is posited on the basis of distributed, decentralized systems: operational nodes — people, things, places, territories — that cooperate freely in order to be more efficient. The outcome of such attempts is hybrid or multifunctional spaces that perform in a dynamic way according to their qualities.

LIVING LANDSCAPES

URBAN GREEN

BIG INFRASTRUCTURES

ENERGY SYSTEMS

PARAMETRIC URBANISM

SOCIAL & COLLABORATIVE

THEORIES & STRATEGIES

WATERWHEEL

Enriquez Lage Juan

juanenriquezlage@gmail.com

Spain

The project is placed in Almada, in the Tajo river estuary, in front of Lisbon . The setting is full of old factories and warehouses related to the activity of the river. Due to a pronounced topography, the site is isolated of the whole city (there is a height difference of 35 m. between the city and the coast) that provoques a lack of identity.

The proposal will try to evidence the possibilities of a river to regenerate its environment, improving the activities and systems related to an estuary. This projects could be used as a reference for any hydraulical centres in any estuary. In this case, the choice of the situation (next to the big concrete hollow), will emphasize and turn it into a new landmark in Almada , providing a new identity to this place.

The first decision is to study the different kind of relations between land- water along the coast. The portuguese waterwheels are taken as a conceptual reference, using the tides to produce hydraulic energy. The building is sited inside the river in order to define a new limit in the riverfront and to create a public space related to water.

A deep study of the tides and water currents show us that the current has two directions, depending on the ocean tide. When the tide is rising, the oceanic water goes into the estuary pushing the river current. On the other hand, when the ocean tide is decreasing, the river current has its natural direction. These particularities will let us take the opportunity of using the water and the tides to produce energy, like a traditional waterwheel. Moreover, the use of a correct natural ventilation and the energy produced by the turbines let the building be self-sufficient ...

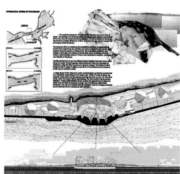

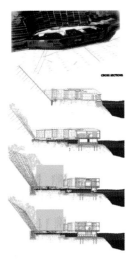

CROSS SECTIONS

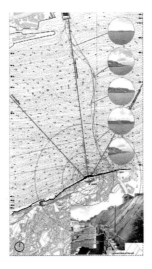

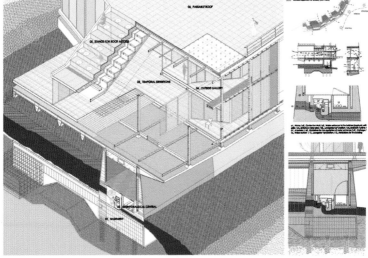

01_ PASSABLE ROOF

02_ STANDS FOR ROOF ACCESS

03_ TEMPORAL EXHIBITIONS

04_ OUTSIDE GALLERY

METEOROLOGICAL CENTRAL

05_ BASEMENT

Air-Conditioned Rooms
Non Air-Conditioned Paths
Outside Openes: Air Gallery (self-vent)

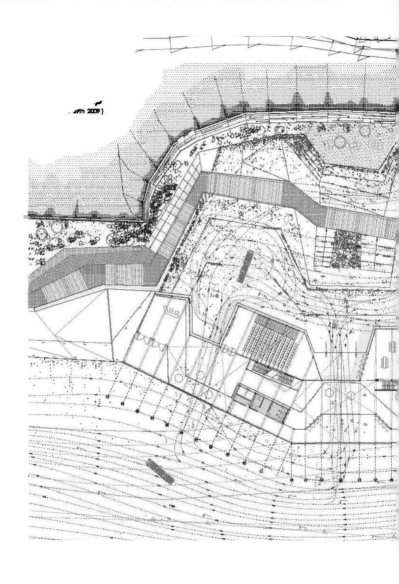

LIVING LANDSCAPES

URBAN GREEN

BIO INFRASTRUCTURES

ENERGY SYSTEMS

PARAMETRIC URBANISM

SOCIAL & COLLABORATIVE

THEORIES & STRATEGIES

HOLE CITY *FINALIST*

Ventura Blanch Ferran
Carlos Almansa Ballesteros

ferranventura@msn.com

Spain

This project is proposing new models of cities. Cities which are more respectful with the environment and society. Risky and experimental cities, which are seeking out to understand a Nature and Territory that have improved with natural high technologies and ancient wisdom. The wind / wind power, the sun / solar energy, the ground / thermal inertia, water / climatic conditioner, people / social relationships, technology / new possibilities, solid waste / biomass energy, grey water / irrigation, these are some of the concepts to be implemented into the project for the generation of a new urban environment. In order to bring out these new conditions we develop a building which is continually interacting with its interior courtyard. A public space that is managed by a large interactive tree that creates the ideal conditions bother for the courtyard and the whole block of houses. This is an architecture looking for the connection and harmony with adjacent urban and rural territory.

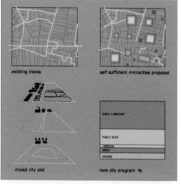

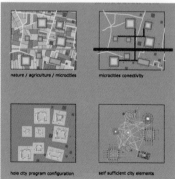

LIVING LANDSCAPES

URBAN GREEN

BIO INFRASTRUCTURES

ENERGY SYSTEMS

PARAMETRIC URBANISM

SOCIAL & COLLABORATIVE

THEORIES & STRATEGIES

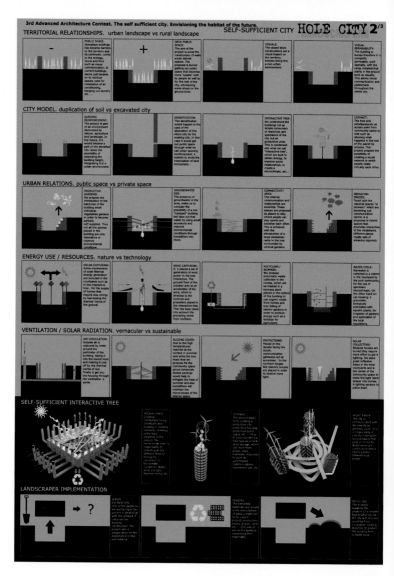

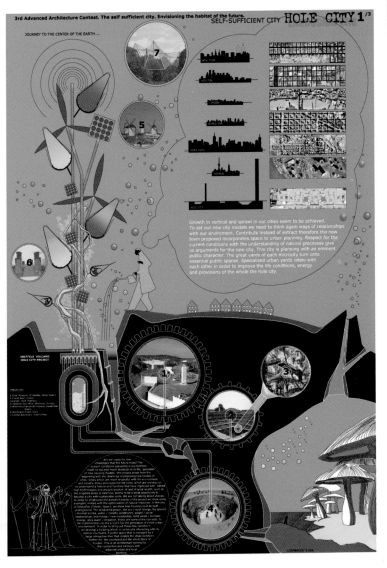

LIVING LANDSCAPES

URBAN GREEN

BIO INFRASTRUCTURES

ENERGY SYSTEMS

PARAMETRIC URBANISM

SOCIAL & COLLABORATIVE

THEORIES & STRATEGIES

3rd Advanced Architecture Contest. The self sufficient city. Envisioning the habitat of the future.

SELF-SUFFICIENT CITY HOLE CITY 1/3

JOURNEY TO THE CENTER OF THE EARTH....

Growth in vertical and sprawl in our cities seem to be achieved. To set out new city models we need to think again ways of relationships with our enviroment. Contribute instead of extract therefore the new town proposed incorporates space to urban planning. Respect for the current conditions with the understanding of natural processes give us arguments for the new city. This city is planning with an eminent public character. The great yards of each microcity turn onto essential public spaces. Specialized urban yards relate with each other in order to improve the life conditions, energy and provisions of the whole the hole city.

SNEFFELS VOLCANO. HOLE CITY PROJECT

223

CONTINUOUS CITY: COMBUSTING DATA CAPITAL

Videmsky Laci
Kevin Lee

videmsky@siteunseen.org

United States

Continuous City, a collaborative research and design project, seeks to redefine and recast infrastructure within a global system of flows, where physical form is mediated by interactions with complex behavioral systems, such as oscillations in politics, markets, populations, and habitation trends. Rather than assuming its traditional role as intervention or support, we contend that a new infrastructure strategy might better reflect and respond to a post-Fordist logistical landscape than the inadequate status quo. Assembled with the awareness of a deeper ecological order that considers energy and waste, resource scarcity, and shifting economies, the new infrastructure we explore registers these global pressures and the region's fluctuating networks.

Continuous City surveys how data centers relate to patterns of urbanism and climate change in two ways; Examines how we may coexist with infrastructure in a dense, vertical arrangement, exploiting the potential for specific infrastructural typologies to participate in a continuum of energy exchange, becoming the

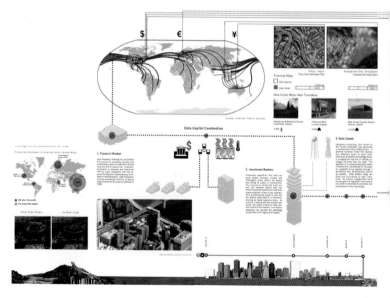

224

substrate for the creation of new civic habitation and ritual; Proposes the conflation of public and private infrasatructure as a strategy that mobilizes perpetually hamstrung public sector ventures, while simultaneously energizing the inertial slip-stream of private infrastructural development; Envisions a lifestyle that extends the interior of the enclosure to the immediate neighborhood vicinity, advocating hybrid use where the domains of public and private blend naturally; Proposes a new taxonomy of open space, where the status, definition, and traditional preservation of nature are reoriented.

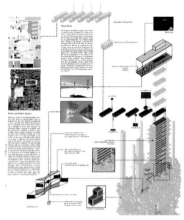

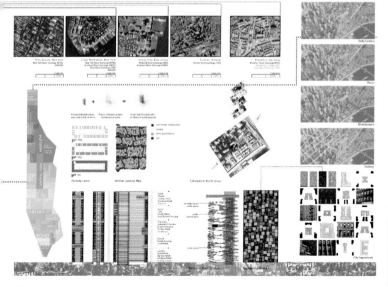

THE WAFFLE HOUSE

Tsai Tsunghan

ajtsai@arch.nctu.edu.tw

Taiwan

Global warming already is the relevant issue around the world, Taiwan is located in subtropical, tropical and crowded area, the urban heat island effect will become even more significant issue in the future. HsinChu City, located along the north-western coast of Taiwan, has shown an increase in temperature at a rate 60% faster then the world average temperature gain, and is therefore the most affected area of the world. The phenomena reflecting on the major Disaster of Taiwan.

The campus space is design as model example, through the Profiles of observation of urban areas. Discuss about the dynamic system mechanism of intervention, dealing with interface between artificial and nature of conflict relations and possibility.

The new building on campus provides a new typology and form that integrates the relationship between Architecture, landscape and Infrastructure.

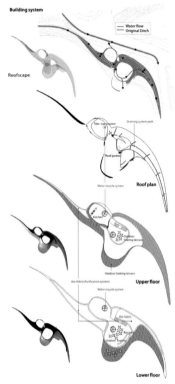

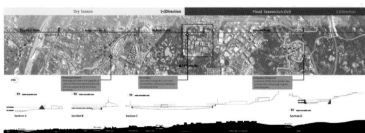

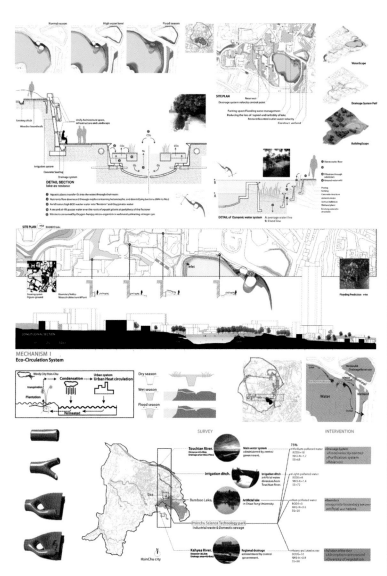

LIVING LANDSCAPES

URBAN GREEN

BIO INFRASTRUCTURES

ENERGY SYSTEMS

PARAMETRIC URBANISM

SOCIAL & COLLABORATIVE

THEORIES & STRATEGIES

WaterScape

Drainage System Perf

BuildingScape

SITE PLAN

Reservoir

Drainage system velocity control points
Parking space/Flooding water management
Reducing the loss of topsoil and turbidity of lake
Restore&control water velocity
Construct wetland

DETAIL SECTION
lake as restorer

1. Aquatic plants transfer O_2 into the water through their roots
2. Nutrients flow downward through media containing heterotrophic and denitrifying bacteria (NH4 to No.)
3. An lift raises high BOD water into "Restorer" and Oxygenate water
4. A second air lift passes water over the roots of aquatic plants at periphery of the Restorer
5. Nitrate is consumed by Oxygen-hungry micro-organism in sediments releasing nitrogen gas

DETAIL of Dynamic water system   A: average water line
B: Flood line

- Storm water flow
- Filtration through substrates
- Ground water rate

Paving
Setting
Concrete structure
semisteel media
tortus buffalose
Wetland plant
Existing concrete structure

SITE PLAN BAMBOO lake

Drainage system
Figure-ground

Boundary Study
Water/Architecture &Plant

inlet

Flooding Prediction +4m

LONGITUDINAL SECTION

MECHANISM I
Eco-Circulation System

Windy City Hsin-Chu

Condensation → Urban system
Urban Heat circulation

transpiration
Plantation
Permeated

Dry season
Wet season
Flood season

Water

Wetland&
Drainage Reservoir

Wetland
Outlet

SURVEY

INTERVENTION

Touchian River.
Distance=45.64km
Drainage area=86.7km2

Main water system
administered by central
government.

73%

>Medium-polluted water
BOD5=16
NH3-N=1.2
SS=68

>Drainage system
>Flood velocity control
>Purification system
>Reservoir

Irrigation ditch.

Irrigation ditch
artificial water
diversion from
Touchian River.

>Light-polluted water
BOD5=8
NH3-N=1.4
SS=72

Bamboo Lake.

Artificial lake
in Chiao Tung University.

>Num-polluted water
BOD5=4
NH3-N=0.5
SS=20

>Boundary
unspecific boundary between
artificial and nature.

Hsinchu Science Technology park
Industrial waste & Domestic sewage

Kehyea River.
Distance=36.2km
Drainage area=46.4km2

regional drainage
administered by central
government.

>Heavy-polluted water
BOD5=33
NH3-N=3.9
SS=90

>Pollution of the river
>Absorption rate control
>Diversity of vegetation

Site

HsinChu city

ORGANIC FUTURISTIC PHENOMENON FLOATING CITYBALL

Lee Austmon
Richmon

austmon24@gmail.com

Malaysia

The Organic Floating Cityball and the Magic City (World Cup Building) is designed to generate energy from its outer skin with embedded photo-voltaic cells, collect rain water, and improve the distribution of natural daylight. They are very self-sufficient, making it very sustainable in any lifestyle, eco-friendly, and energy-efficient. Ways of maintaining such a high priority is to adapt the latest technological advancement and expertise to it's' design and building ethics.

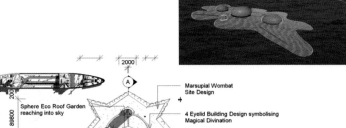

Marsupial Wombat Site Design

Sphere Eco Roof Garden reaching into sky

4 Eyelid Building Design symbolising Magical Divination

Cyclical Access Passage for interconnections

concrete ground

Sphere ball windows symbolising revivalism

ABOVE: SITE PLAN

It's off the coast of Barcelona.

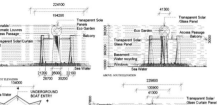

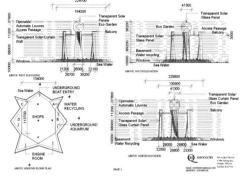

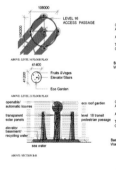

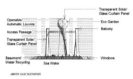

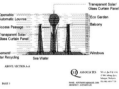

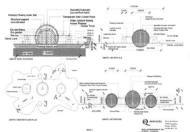

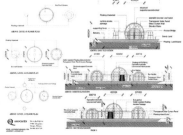

WATER AND THE CITY
COPENHAGEN + HELSINKI

Witkowski Boguslaw
Daniel Gola
Urszula Medes
Dominika Janicka
Tim Thornton
bw@tpda.be

Belgium

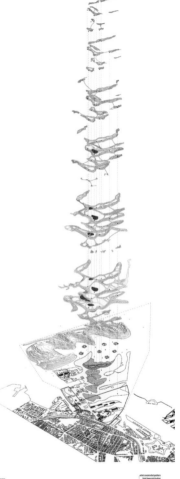

The global warming is the main reason of raising a sea level and a lack of water for domestic use in the near future. It will put underwater the millions of the hectares of land and leave us less and less living space for agriculture and human settlements. Apart of that, the contemporary cities are slowly reaching its limits, the terrains are overused and the constantly growing need for spaces, force us to search for a new way to city expansion. The race to the sky is not the solution. We have some ideas how to solve these burning problems of the present and of the nearest future and how to obtain a dense city without skyscrapers in respect of Mother Nature.

Let us concentrate on two examples of European costal areas which will be very exposed to such kind of problems: Nordhavnen in Copenhagen and Greater Helsinki area.

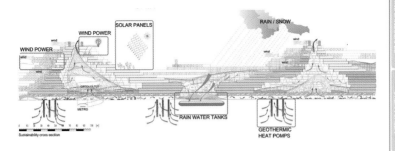

WIND POWER
WIND POWER
SOLAR PANELS
RAIN / SNOW
wind
wind
wind
wind
GREEN FILTER
METRO
RAIN WATER TANKS
GEOTHERMIC HEAT POMPS

Sustainability cross-section

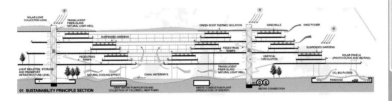

SOLAR LIGHT COLLECTING LENS
TRANSLUCENT FIBER-GLASS NATURAL LIGHT WELL
SUSPENDED GARDENS
GREEN ROOF THERMIC ISOLATION
WIND MILLS
WIND POWER
SUSPENDED GARDENS
SOLAR PANELS (PHOTOVOLTAIC AND HEATING)

LIGHT INDUSTRIE, STORAGE AND TRANSPORT INFRASTRUCTURE LEVEL
PEDESTRIAN RAMPS
NATURAL COOLING EFFECT
CANAL WATERWAY
PEDESTRIAN RAMPS
VERTICAL CIRCULATION
TRANSLUCENT FIBER-GLASS NATURAL LIGHT WELL
CO_2 BIO-FILTERS
PARKINGS

01 SUSTAINABILITY PRINCIPLE SECTION

GREY WATER PURIFICATION AND COLLECTION OF CALORIES (HEAT PUMP)
WASTE COMBUSTION PLANT (PRODUCTION OF ENERGY)
METRO CONNECTION

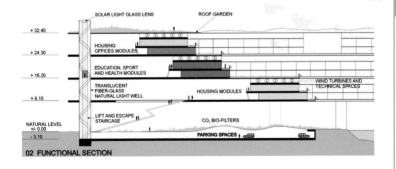

SOLAR LIGHT GLASS LENS
ROOF GARDEN

+ 32.40
HOUSING OFFICES MODULES

+ 24.30
EDUCATION, SPORT AND HEALTH MODULES

+ 16.20
TRANSLUCENT FIBER-GLASS NATURAL LIGHT WELL
HOUSING MODULES
WIND TURBINES AND TECHNICAL SPACES

+ 8.10

NATURAL LEVEL
+/- 0.00
LIFT AND ESCAPE STAIRCASE
CO_2 BIO-FILTERS

- 3.10
PARKING SPACES

02 FUNCTIONAL SECTION

THINK GREEN

LIVING LANDSCAPES
URBAN GREEN
BIO-INFRASTRUCTURES
ENERGY SYSTEMS
PARAMETRIC URBANISM
SOCIAL & COLLABORATIVE
THEORIES & STRATEGIES

LIVING LANDSCAPES

URBAN GREEN

BIO INFRASTRUCTURES

ENERGY SYSTEMS

PARAMETRIC URBANISM

SOCIAL & COLLABORATIVE

THEORIES & STRATEGIES

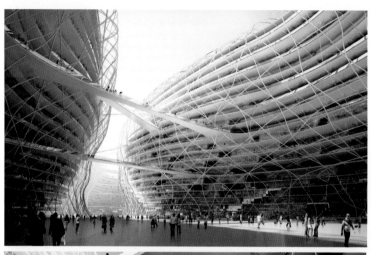

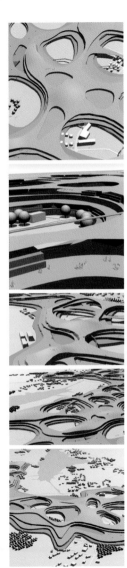

LIVING LANDSCAPES

URBAN GREEN

BIO INFRASTRUCTURES

ENERGY SYSTEMS

PARAMETRIC URBANISM

SOCIAL & COLLABORATIVE

THEORIES & STRATEGIES

HUMANITY'S ANSWER TO NATURE'S QUEST... EDIFICE 2045

Bhadgaonkar Jai
Shirish Parab
Vishal Aher
Dhara Purohit

bhadgaonkarjai@gmail.com

India

With numerous developments and progress being achieved in the 21st century, it remains unobserved rather ignored that there is an equally rather even rapid degradation of the milieu.

On the observed research and analysis the graph of progress is rising for the God's brainy creature and declining for the rest of the terrestrials. A distinct line that goes ignored in the rat race of human progress. With the current rate of degradation the scenario about 50 years down the line only reveals to an inhabitable environment and the Darwin's theory "The survival of the fittest" shall be seen in the dark reality.

Hence, we propose an edifice – The Earth City ... 2045 where humanity is the only religion and the progress graph includes all the living entities. It is an attempt towards using the technology at it's best and in the interest of all.

Here, the technology is developed basis that 'Nature is the Science' and the learning from this science will only bring in development of this paradise – the earth, in it's complete sense.

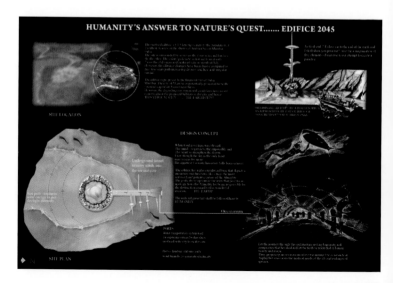

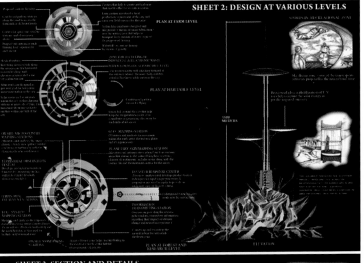

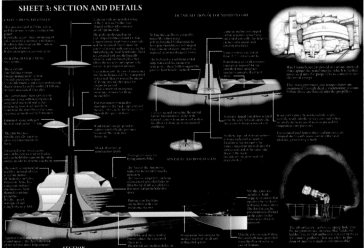

SHAPES OF THE MOUNTAINS

P Diana Carolina

dipebe@gmail.com

Colombia

In Medellín, architects focus their building designs to specific uses, to which the building will respond during its useful life time, affecting their sustainability. Then the buildings:

– Aren't flexible; creating the need for users to get adapted to them, in contraposition of the idea that the buildings are the ones who have to get adapted to the user's needs.

– Become obsolete, when a change in the social or economical dynamics of the neighborhood where they are implanted occurs.

– Create the need of larger displacement of the habitants to get what they need.

– Don't search answers to ecological problems of our world.

As solution, the self sufficient building must respond to two principles:

– Flexible:

Mixed uses

The user can choose the use, area and distribution, by choosing modules.

Adaptability to the change of use and user

– Ecological:

Mixed uses

Productive modules

Rain water recycling

Natural light

Natural ventilation

Solar panels

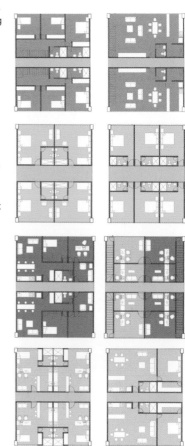

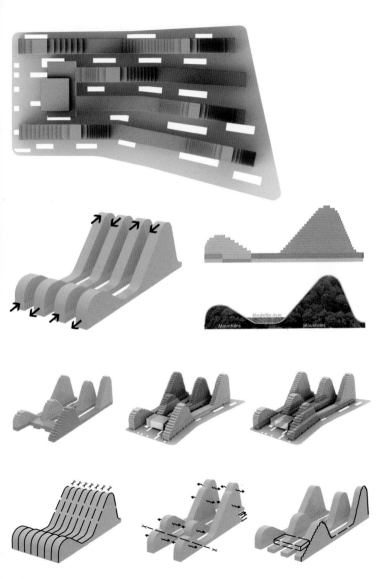

LIVING LANDSCAPES

URBAN GREEN

BIO-INFRASTRUCTURES

ENERGY SYSTEMS

PARAMETRIC URBANISM

SOCIAL & COLLABORATIVE

THEORIES & STRATEGIES

Medellin river

Mountains

Mountains

240

LIVING LANDSCAPES

URBAN GREEN

BIO-INFRASTRUCTURES

ENERGY SYSTEMS

PARAMETRIC URBANISM

SOCIAL & COLLABORATIVE

THEORIES & STRATEGIES

EXTENSION SELF-SUFFICIENT-NETWORKING APPARATUS

Lavoie-Levesque Jonathan
Laurene Bachand
Yoann Plourde
Caroline Chauvel
Jessica Collin-Lacasse

jonaslavoielevesque@hotmail.com

Canada

Self-Sufficient Networking Apparatus is a direct response to the diverse problems observed in the urban landscape. In fact, cities are taking their energy too far away, enclosing green spaces, giving up on their infrastructures and, finally, inevitably spreading out in an out-of-control fashion. In light of these facts, the project has been developed around four relevant themes: a more efficient energy production and distribution, the revaluation of obsolete infrastructures, the implementation of a net-work connecting green spaces and aban-doned lands and the ability for the device to expand following the pace at which the cities grow. The versatile device adapts to its environment, transforming itself to fit the new urban reality. The membrane supports electricity production, yet it acts as a filter to urban pollution and becomes a strong signal to the inhabitants, traveling overhead, creating sporadic events, arous-ing one's interest. In the studied case, two principal sites were chosen: The New York Highline and the abandoned train tunnel going through Harlem (Freedom Tunnel) in New York City. The intervention links both structures and puts emphasis on the rela-tion between similar yet distant entities.

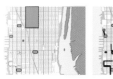

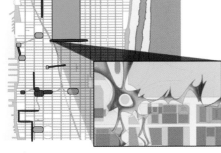

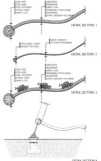

DETAIL SECTION 1

DETAIL SECTION 2

DETAIL SECTION 3

DETAIL SECTION 4

DETAIL PLAN 1

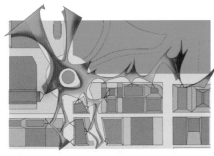 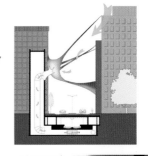

 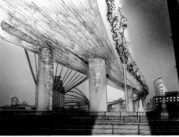

LIVING LANDSCAPES

URBAN GREEN

BG INFRASTRUCTURES

ENERGY SYSTEMS

PARAMETRIC URBANISM

SOCIAL & COLLABORATIVE

THEORIES & STRATEGIES

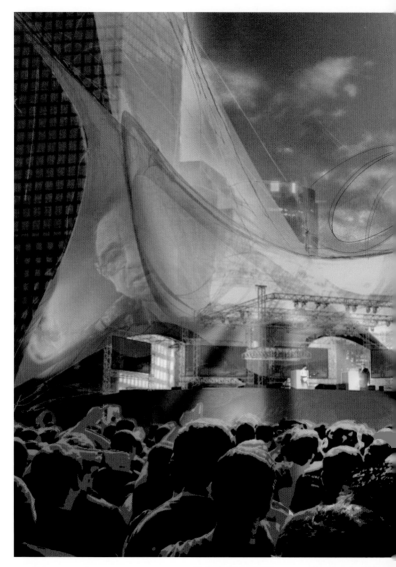

LIVING LANDSCAPES

URBAN GREEN

BIO-INFRASTRUCTURES

ENERGY SYSTEMS

PARAMETRIC URBANISM

SOCIAL & COLLABORATIVE

THEORIES & STRATEGIES

ECOLOGIC URBAN MODEL – AN IDEA OF A CITY

Castillo Serna Julian Eduardo
Martha Ines Sierra

julianecast@yahoo.com

Colombia

This proposal is mainly an "abstract model", a "city pattern" which can become a useful tool for designing ecologically concerned urban environments. As a pattern, it's meant to provide several principles to be applied in different situations and it's flexible enough to be transformed depending on each reality. It can work for redeveloping parts of existing cities, new urban developments and even new cities.

The shape is a consequence of structuring the entire model on pedestrian movements and public transportation. The short measure is the result of the maximum distance (around 500 meters) for reaching the massive transportation stop, which shouldn't take more than 7 minutes. This elongated shape is formed by transverse segments that we call "sectors", which have very high densities

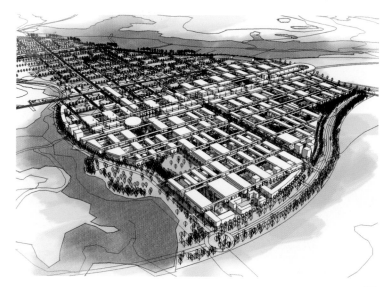

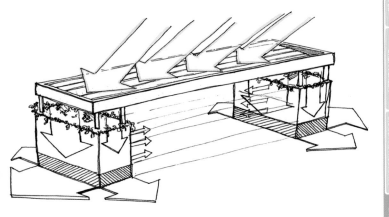

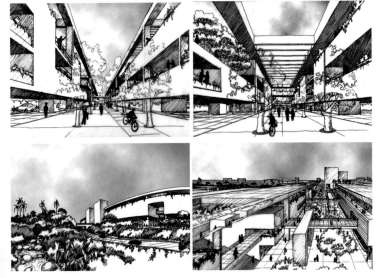

LIVING LANDSCAPES

URBAN GREEN

BIO-INFRASTRUCTURES

ENERGY SYSTEMS

PARAMETRIC URBANISM

SOCIAL & COLLABORATIVE

THEORIES & STRATEGIES

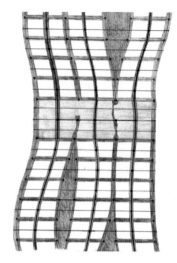

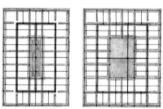

in order to provide a complex and diverse environment, in contrast to the dispersed and wasteful pattern of present cities. Each sector is composed by "strips" which contain most of the urban activities but in certain proportions, responding to the concept of micro-zoning. The strip becomes also the basic unit of metabolic functioning of the city to generate a more rational, moderate and less expensive management of energy resources as well as waste production and therefore increasing its local self-sufficiency. For each strip, there is a structure that "precedes" and supports individual architecture (the same as the streets do)

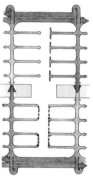

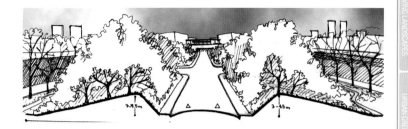

which we call Environmental Supports.
These supports are composed by large
technical roofs for collecting solar energy,
column-ducts carrying cables and pipe-
lines which distribute electric energy and
hot water or hot fluid for heating/cooling
purposes, and a technical basement for
water and solid waste treatment.
The continuous green spaces network
takes part of the environmental supports
system with its environmental protection zones, where final water treatment
is done. It also serves for diminishing
car noise and pollution and improving air
quality and temperature conditions.

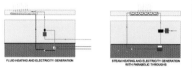

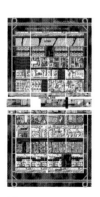

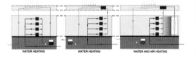

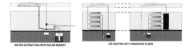

LIVING LANDSCAPES

URBAN GREEN

BIO-INFRASTRUCTURES

ENERGY SYSTEMS

PARAMETRIC URBANISM

SOCIAL & COLLABORATIVE

THEORIES & STRATEGIES

CONSTANTA CITY

Comanescu Raluca Daniela

lalneagra@gmail.com

Romania

The intervention on the city Constanta (Romania) is planned for a medium to long period of time
The main key concepts of the project :
THE AGRICULTURE CITY = an agricultural spine is to be implemented in middle town and represent the primary area to supply ecological food for our daily life and to became a a fusion between the nature benefits and human capacities
A new complex of social houses built accordingly to the "passive house"

concept will be the habitat for people with low income.
A new water channel will allows an ecological transportation with small solar boats and it will be the principal source of water for houses ventilation system with heat recovery using ground heat exchanger (Geo-exchange system)
THE HIGH INTELLIGENT DRIVING = the concept of producing energy using car movement. The more cars in traffic, the more energy will be generated.

Self sufficient city - Detailing the High Inteligent Driving

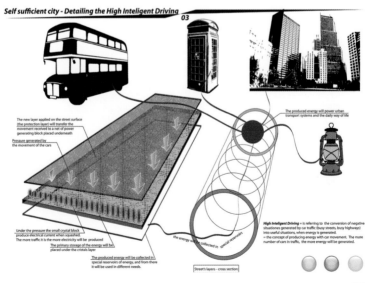

03

The new layer applied on the street surface (the protection layer) will transfer the movement received to a net of power generating block placed underneath

Pressure generated by the movement of the cars

The produced energy will power urban transport systems and the daily way of life

Under the pressure the small crystal block produce electrical current when squashed. The more traffic it is the more electricity will be produced

The primary storage of the energy will be placed under the cristals layer

The produced energy will be collected in special reservoirs of energy, and from there it will be used in different needs.

the energy will be collected in special reservoirs

High Inteligent Driving = is referring to the conversion of negative situationes generated by car traffic (busy streets, busy highways) into useful situations, when energy is generated.
= the concept of producing energy with car movement. The more number of cars in traffic, the more energy will be generated.

Street's layers - cross section

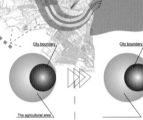

In the context of global warming and the lack of vital resources, our main ideas must focus on reduction of the impact on the planet from urban consumption patterns. Therefore we should promote the idea od the city that it powers itself entirely by means of renewable energy systems.

The purpose of the project is to find solutions to convert Constanta City (Romania) from a threat to the nature to a self sufficient city. The project is planned for a medium to long period of time (50 - 80 years)

The main key concepts of the project are:
1. THE AGRICULTURE CITY
2. THE HIGH INTELIGENT DRIVING

Future boundary of the city
City boundary

Future boundary of the city
City boundary

The new spine of the city:
The agricultural spine

City boundary

The agricultural area

City boundary

In present Constanta is one of the most bigest cities in Romania, that leaves a big ecological footprint on the global environment. It is a big energy consumer and because the large amount of waste it is a threath to the nature. Latest studies had announce a new expansion of the city's boundary. To avoid the development of this enemy of the nature, we should act now.

Stage one:
The agricultural spine = the primary area to supply the food and material we usually need in our daily life.
= the power of agriculture in the process of self-sufficiency
= the power of the nature will grow if human slows than
= a fusion between the nature benefits (agriculture) and human capacities (inventing the passive house system)

Stage two:
The spine will have a big influence in the development of city's new areas: the agricultural spine will enclose the old urban area

Stage three:
The old area will finish included into the new ecological spine.
The old area will soon change his character and will share the same ecological orientation of the spine.
So it will born the agricultural city

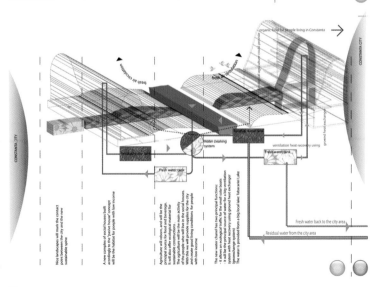

Nice landscapes will mark the contact point between the city and the new sustainable spine

A new complex of social houses built accordingly to the "passive house" concept will be the habitat for people with low income

Agriculture will reborn, and will be the principal source for food and beverage. It will also offer ecological material for sustainable construction.
The agriculture will be the main activity of the people who will live in the social houses. With this we will provide supplies for the city and create good living conditions for people with low income

The new water channel has two principal functions:
- it allows an ecological traffic, for the small boats
- it will be the principal source of water for a big ventilation system (with heat recovery using ground heat exchanger (geoexchange system)
The water is provided from a big local lake Tabacariei Lake

Fresh water back to the city area

Residual water from the city area

RAINING BUILDING

Vanzato Nicolas
Jean-Fran

nicovanzato@gmail.com

France

We considered global warming as a migration of local climates.
Chile appears as an extreme climatic object, the collage of strongly contrasted environments: ocean, high mountains, and lush forest amongst an extremely arid desert, self maintaining in condensing fog. Santiago is the sprawling capital, with heavy traffic, smog and air pollution. Rain remains the most efficient agent to counter pollution.

The project is a building to bring down the rain.

The envelope is a refreshing skin composed of humidity sensors. Like the forest in the desert, it catches vaporous water from surroundings. Water is lead to a tank via an hydroelectric station. The electrolyzed water tank produces hydrogen, injected in a h engine. Both systems generate oxygen spread in the atmosphere. The buildings stand nearby critical traffic zones, likely to release rainfalls, limiting pollution peaks; and take presence of an urban abstract sculpture related to mountainous landscape and the sky.

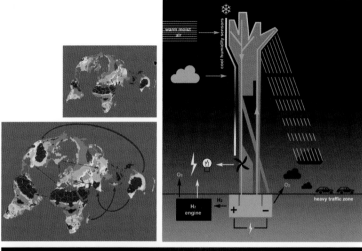

LIVING LANDSCAPES

URBAN GREEN

BIO-INFRASTRUCTURES

ENERGY SYSTEMS

PARAMETRIC URBANISM

SOCIAL & COLLABORATIVE

THEORIES & STRATEGIES

LIVING LANDSCAPES

URBAN GREEN

BIO INFRASTRUCTURES

ENERGY SYSTEMS

PARAMETRIC URBANISM

SOCIAL & COLLABORATIVE

THEORIES & STRATEGIES

URBAN CORRIDOR

Bj Osmann
Christian Kreiselmaier

osmannbjoern@hotmail.com

Germany

What is the concept of the city for the next century?
What kind of need's has the future city to perform that will develop nowaday's cities?
These are the questions for sufficient and innovative town planning.
To achiev these goal's you have to reduce the planing processs to the fundamental basic of society.
Breaking border`s
The territorial conflict potential worldwide is today as current as it was centuries ago. Nowadys economic reasons are more complex as they used to be. In times of total globalization these patterns of conflict potential appear antiquated and as a relict of power that schould be transcended.

The global city
Common projects of states with aggression potential are a step forward for intercultural exchange and pacifying for enemies of the past.
The city will be a place of convergency for topics like politics, culture, religion and social engagement.
It will be a platform for education and sensitisation, a marketplace even for the smallest part of different civilizations.

LIVING LANDSCAPES

URBAN GREEN

BIO INFRASTRUCTURES

ENERGY SYSTEMS

PARAMETRIC URBANISM

SOCIAL & COLLABRATIVE

THEORIES & STRATEGIES

Bring peace

The example for urban planning is the territorial conflict betwenn north- and south korea. An urban corridor connects the two states throughout the demilitarized zone between the countries. This town planning gesture will activate the potential for both countries in the field of economy, social maintenance and every day life.

urban corridor

Energie extraction:

The global city should be also a ecological signal example.

Earth

A geothermale power station extractet warm air. The exceed warm air will be redirected in a wind channel.

Air

The to the top streaming warm air powered a huge wind turbine in the crystals.

Sun

The facade from the crystals are completed construted with photovoltaik pannels.

Elemental city

The global city doesn`t need extern Energie sources. It recieve all it´s Energy requirement from natural power plants.

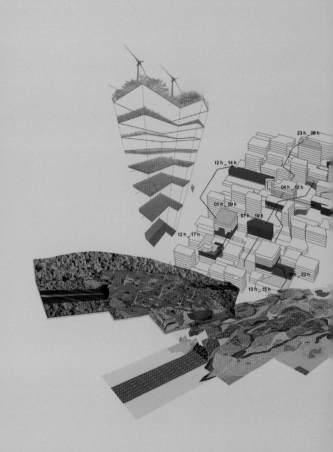

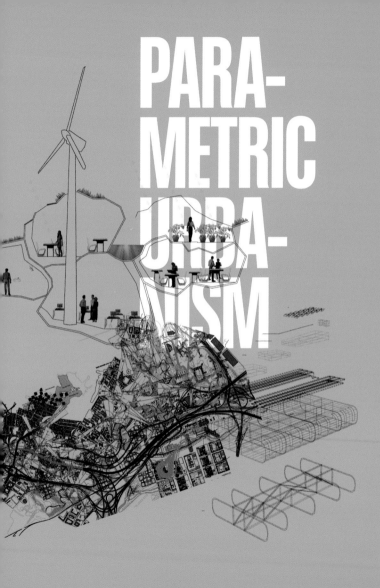

PARA-METRIC URBA-NISM

LIVING LANDSCAPES

URBAN GREEN

BIO INFRASTRUCTURES

ENERGY SYSTEMS

PARAMETRIC URBANISM

SOCIAL & COLLABORATIVE

THEORIES & STRATEGIES

PARAMETRIC URBANISM

Projects that propose cities as an environment-adaptive mechanism
Recognizing that the idea of change is an essential characteristic of cities, associative urbanism explores responsive and adaptive design systems shifted up to the urban scale. The vision of the city of the future can be described as an adaptive model of ecology, an environmental and cultural hub capable of generating eventual growth by means of its own collective intelligence and internal regulations.

The digital tools are used both to analyse existing urban conditions and to produce the city mechanism that collects information (forces and effects) from the external source of human occupation and local landscape. We have long since gone beyond the perception that master-planning should deploy a final state of a form or of a system. The complexity of our cities calls for intelligent, flexible and adaptive new forms of urbanism and urban aesthetics. What future cities need is a master plan capable of being revised over time in response to existing needs and requirements.

By means of bottom-up processes and non-linear systems, through code-based design methods, the future city model is presented as a grid mechanism that cannot be ordered or controlled: instead, it continuously responds and adapts to human and environmental needs. As a result there are no longer independent buildings and infrastructures but habitable organisms and structures that form the nodes of a decentralized network of linked parameters — a network in which each node has its own intelligence and develops its own adaptive behaviour.

The potential of associative tools increases when these are considered and used as the means of creating systems which the users can manipulate within certain parameters. The interaction between user and parametric system takes associative urban planning beyond form and aesthetics. Cities need to be approached with wide-ranging analytical intentions, not based on random processes of generating form. Understanding the context, simulating the city's growth and analysing hidden logics from existing processes of self-organization are powerful actions that open up new possibilities for rethinking our cities and achieving design proposals for dynamic, adaptive and functional city models.

LIVING LANDSCAPES

URBAN GREEN

BIO INFRASTRUCTURES

ENERGY SYSTEMS

PARAMETRIC URBANISM

SOCIAL & COLLABORATIVE

THEORIES & STRATEGIES

SUPER MANGROVESCAPE PRO-RESORT URBANISM

Chen Jung Liu
Yang-Sheng Chen
Tammy_liou@hotmail.com

Taiwan, Province of China

This project is an pro-resort urbanism aims to prevent the new tourist city getting damaged form an inappropriate development which reduce the value of natural landscape, giving a aesthetical plan for the places, while developing form rural to new resort city.

We proposes a new type of tourist resort, which can play as a machine to support self-sufficient system in larger scale, it also integrates the infrastructure of the city before planning, and coherences the social relationship between the local and tourists.

In Alagoas, Brazil. Mangrove is the most symbolic environmental form the local landscape. The mangrove could be the base of water purification system, the resources of local food, energy, also nursing mangrove forest could be high-value agricultural practice for local people. The act of mangrove recovery is a best way to promote eco-tourism for resorts and reduces the land swallowed form the second house developments.

These both win mangrove-base urban plan pursuits the better urban condition for future development.

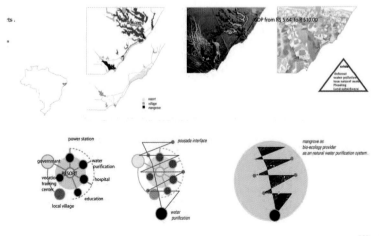

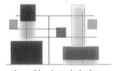

freamwork and basic technical program

mangrove growth and water purify

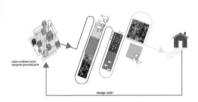

water purification point
mangrove generated point

sewage water

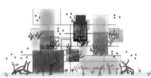

mangrove transplant and space release

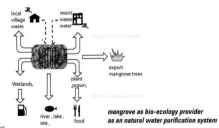

local
village
waste

resort
waste
water

collect input and factor

export
mangrove trees

Wetlands,

plant
,prawn,

river , lake ,
sea ,

food

produce local and factor

**mangrove as bio-ecology provider
as an natural water purification system**

water purification point
mangrove generated point

mangrove nursery

sewage water

LIVING LANDSCAPES

URBAN GREEN

BIO-INFRASTRUCTURES

ENERGY SYSTEMS

PARAMETRIC URBANISM

SOCIAL & COLLABORATIVE

THEORIES & STRATEGIES

LIVING LANDSCAPES

URBAN GREEN

BIO INFRASTRUCTURES

ENERGY SYSTEMS

PARAMETRIC URBANISM

SOCIAL & COLLABORATIVE

THEORIES & STRATEGIES

CITY FACTORY

 FINALIST

Fernandez Francisco

deabrugorri@hotmail.com

Venezuela

The barrio of Maracaibo due to its newness lacks programs different from the domestic one. City factory becomes a multifunctional piece that provides these settlements the minimal conditions necessary to overcoming poverty, turning the community into a functional piece of the city and not another problem within the local urbanity.

The maximum problem of any informal settlement is its ignorance on the needs of the society. City Factory is shown as the one piece that without disturbing the state of the place, inserts within it an accumulation of programs that set out to drive the end of poverty of which they live in these domestic conglomerates, without objections on age or racial term.

The City factory proposes a system where educating initiates a relation between social and economic dynamics which allows the person to depend exclusively on oneself.

By all this, the intention of this intervention is to promote the self-sufficiency in social terms, making of the underprivileged population indelible actors of the urban dynamics, which would take them to surpass their stage of poverty.

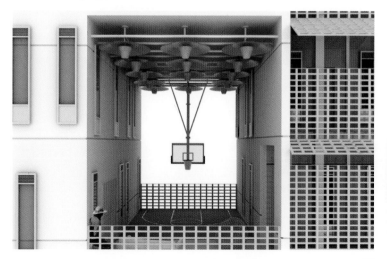

Program without age

The maximum problem of any informal settlement is its ignorance on the needs of the society. CITY FACTORY is shown as the one place that without disturbing the state of the place, inserts within it an accumulation of **PROGRAMS THAT SET OUT TO DRIVE THE END OF POVERTY** of which they live in these domestic conglomerates, without objections on age or racial terms.

Poverty. A problem of et etc.

The world-wide problem of poverty as made evident when finding ourselves with an economic crises like the one currently taken place. Proposing a massive equipment within so precarious zones only tries to break a cycle that affects all the inhabitants of the settlements, and that cause today's service problems to become tomorrow's national crises.

Components
The elements that form the construction are based on the local schemes, where a primary structure (1) will give support to a vast composition by very slight and precarious elements (2) in which the content appears much disorganized, (3) a characterize the essence of the local housing, in this case translated to CITY FACTORY.

Ciudad Lossada.
Latitud: 10°41'41.95"N
Longitud: 71°38'28.20"W

FACTS

98,5%
population under the line of poverty.

1,2%
Houses with at least 1 formalized basic service.

76,1%
unemployment or informal labor circles.

58,6%
51% come from ethnic groups or has native ancestry

95,5%
buildings with domestic program only.

The exhibition of these numbers makes convincing the critical problem that initiated on this population, since their conditions lead them to see themselves surrounded in a cycle that will only bring larger poverty levels.

The situation of the informal habitat has been so relegated in the political and social agenda in our region that this investigation had to raise the planimetry displayed here due to its total nonexistence.

Data taken from INE

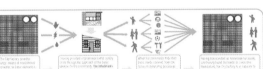

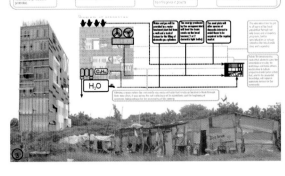

Water and gas will be provided by a water treatment plant that feeds a well and a tank of biomass (1 or 2 domestic gas cylinders)

The energy produced by the aerogenerator will feed the basic needs on the local housing (1 or 2 domestic light bulbs)

The seed plots will alter species of domestic interest to avoid have to be acquired in the regular market

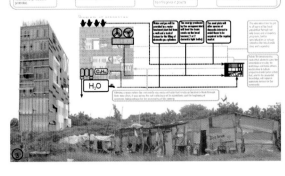

LIVING LANDSCAPES
URBAN GREEN
BIO INFRASTRUCTURES
ENERGY SYSTEMS
PARAMETRIC URBANISM
SOCIAL & COLLABORATIVE
THEORIES & STRATEGIES

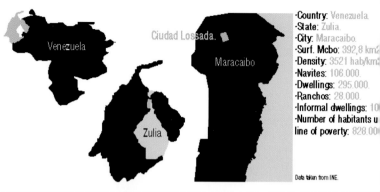

- **Country:** Venezuela.
- **State:** Zulia.
- **City:** Maracaibo.
- **Surf. Mcbo:** 392,8 km2
- **Density:** 3521 hab/km2
- **Navites:** 106.000.
- **Dwellings:** 295.000.
- **Ranchos:** 28.000.
- **Informal dwellings:** 10
- **Number of habitants u
- **line of poverty:** 828.00

Ciudad Lossada.

Venezuela

Maracaibo

Zulia

Data taken from INE.

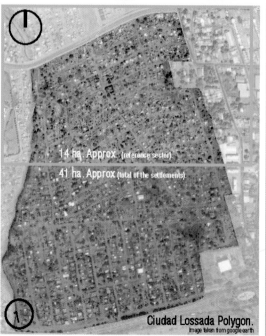

14 ha. Approx. (reference sector)

41 ha. Approx (total of the settlements).

Ciudad Lossada Polygon.
Image taken from google earth

Barrio localization.

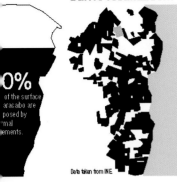

0%
of the surface
aracaibo are
posed by
rmal
ements.

Data taken from INE

MARACAIBO POSSES THE LARGEST PROPORTION OF INFORMAL SURFACE ENROLLED WITHIN A SINGLE URBAN POLYGONAL IN VENEZUELA, with reservation of the Caracas' barrios or paulistas favelas, many of these areas are of recent occupation and LACK IN THEIR MAJORITY OF THE SERVICES AND MINIMUM URBAN SYSTEMS. The land invasions have guaranteed to the more impoverished classes a constant access to the self-constructed housing, this dynamic has solved the problem of the habitat, but it has not guaranteed the existence of the programmatic multiplicity that characterizes the city, turning them into mere grouping of houses and FORCING ITS INHABITANTS TO GO TO THE FORMAL CITY IN SEARCH OF THE NONEXISTENT SERVICES IN THE AREA.

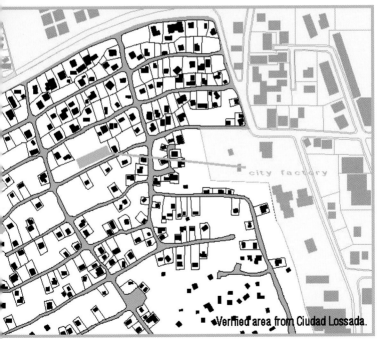

city factory

• Verified area from Ciudad Lossada.

LIVING LANDSCAPES

URBAN GREEN

BIO-INFRASTRUCTURES

ENERGY SYSTEMS

PARAMETRIC URBANISM

SOCIAL & COLLABORATIVE

THEORIES & STRATEGIES

ENVIRONMENTAL_HUB

Kerechanin Adam
Natalie Cregar
Johanna McCrehan
akerech@clemson.edu

United States

Overview of project, including tourism
Tourists continually occupy the city of Barcelona. Between the tourists and natives, the population of Barcelona fluxes seasonally. Typically, natives choose to leave the city when most tourists are entering. The dynamic created is one of sharing. For environmental_HUB, we chose to focus on this interaction by utilizing the 'city exchange' to help lower energy consumption in the city with a new kind of habitat.

Observing the types of places each group primarily uses generates the program for the environment. This includes looking at overlaps as well as their yearly occupation within the city.

Interactivity and Sustainable Elements

The site is situated in an industrial area of the port, which is a rapidly growing tourist area. This is because of the large amounts of tourists that arrive by cruise boats.
To take advantage of the growing debate on public space and sustainability, we designed an area with the goal of making it completely carbon neutral.

Shown below are different areas of the site where energy recycling takes place. This includes wind turbines and solar panels for energy, and rainwater collection for non-potable water. The effect of the rapidly growing water shortage in Barcelona also became an important factor in design. We chose to utilize the silos on site and researched desalination techniques for reusable seawater.

Other energy saving methods includes those powered by the user. Some would be passive for the occupant, like turnstiles and slot machine levers.

A rocky landscape transcends from the mountain to the sea, created from applying a fractal method for structure. The occupant would experience these fractals within the building in the floor forms, and the shape enables the circulation of water and energy throughout the site

Tourism + sustainability

The breakdown of the site shows the same programmatic elements of the city within this habitat powered by its occupants. The diagrammatic approach of this project allowed for a more in depth study of the potential the site holds for sustainable solutions. environmental_HUB creates a place where tourists and locals can cooperate for the betterment of the city.

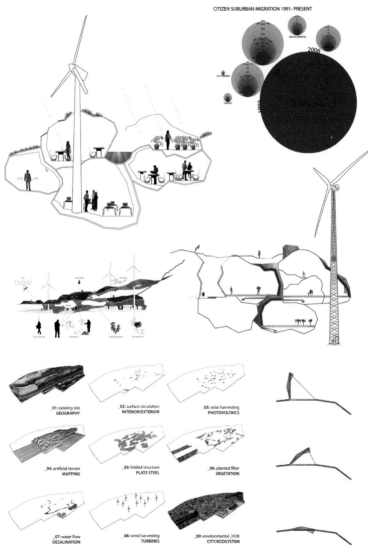

CITIZEN SUBURBAN MIGRATION 1991- PRESENT

VALLÈS ORIENTAL

2006

ALT PENEDES

BARCELONA

2001

GARRAF

_01: existing site
GEOGRAPHY

_02: surface circulation
INTERIOR/EXTERIOR

_03: solar harvesting
PHOTOVOLTAICS

_04: artificial terrain
MAPPING

_05: folded structure
PLATE STEEL

_06: planted filter
VEGETATION

_07: water flow
DESALINATION

_08: wind harvesting
TURBINES

_09: environmental_HUB
CITY/ECOSYSTEM

LIVING LANDSCAPES

URBAN GREEN

BIO-INFRASTRUCTURES

ENERGY SYSTEMS

PARAMETRIC URBANISM

SOCIAL & COLLABORATIVE

THEORIES & STRATEGIES

NON STOP CITY

Magro Baroni Cristina
Virginia Moreno de Dios
Eliana Mangione
Beatriz Mart
Fernando Martínez Goyanes
Methus Srisuchart

cristina.magro@gmail.com

Spain

The main concepts of this self-sufficient city are a consequence of the reflection of the notion of time and its influence in the different lifestyles, interpersonal relationships and its resultant modifications in the residential structure.

The "non-stop city" is defined as that one in which the spaces remain untied from a use segmented in time. The different temporary lines interlace forming a matrix of constant activities, in which the spaces of social relation are not closed circles, but multifunctional containers that encourage meeting through the spatial overlapping of the different activities. It's a city with a new notion of time, without a time-zone, with no imposed schedules, no time limits, a 24 hour city, "a city that never sleeps". It's a globalized city, integrated into a non-stop society.

Non-Stop City:
- matrix of activities
- multifunctional spaces
- 24 hour uses
- compact city

The update of the concept of space-time as a boundary goes through its dissolution in the condensation of the activity

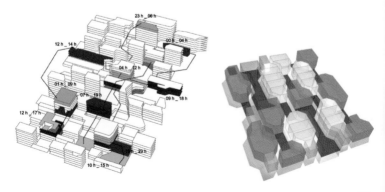

LIVING LANDSCAPES

URBAN GREEN

BIO-INFRASTRUCTURES

ENERGY SYSTEMS

PARAMETRIC URBANISM

SOCIAL & COLLABORATIVE

THEORIES & STRATEGIES

at any point, in which different times are overlapped. The time map gathers in sectors of times, organizing the activity sections that in relation shape the lines of constant activity that characterize the "non-stop-city". This interrelation of activities and uses is established by means of four principal groups: working, eating, resting and playing.

The organization of activities is established according to the sedentary or the nomadic condition of the user. The trend of residential permanency and the different degrees of inflexibility in the habits of the developed activities are responsible of structuring the different uses in the building, which is formed as a system of components.

Its architecture of the non-stop city will be that one where the limits of every individual unit adapt and deform according to the use. These contours will be virtual and changeable, creating a continuous transformation in the city.

The organization of the activities in time, the different time lines of the users as well as the conditions in which the activities are developed, conform the catalogue of pieces / containers that give solution to both, the individual and the collective needs of the tenants of the building. The selection of the integral pieces of the residential public - private space / individual - collective of every user, as well as its location along the infrastructural system form the final solution of the building, adapting it to the specific conditions in every space and in every moment.

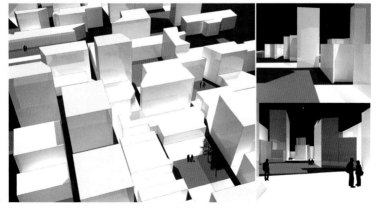

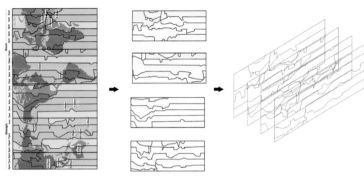

virtual division of time-function-space   overlapped time zone sections   interrelation between sections

The built-up solution is organized by means of an infrastructural system. Its typological response in every situation tries to adapt the characteristics of the use programmed for every zone of activity. Divided in continuous, discontinuous and isolated infrastructures, they appear as virtual limits that are connected to the domestic units selected by the user. The bend/ fold of the infrastructures answer to the spatial characteristics required by the contained uses.

Non-stop city is the stratification of multi-function container spaces which are interconnected through time and space, and which meet the expectations of the matrix. The dwellings of this city should respond to this multi-time concept, where the border between each individual unit will adapt and deform according to the use it contains. These borders are virtual and always changing, creating a continuous transformation of the city.

An infrastructural system shapes both the edges and the connections of the general scheme of the building, to which the elements of use developed in the shape of a catalogue are connected. Custom made dwellings chosen from an online catalogue, allowing the selection and location of the pieces along the infrastructure. The relation between space and time by means of the new technologies applied to communication, transport, relations, etc., appears as an intermediate point in the process of condensation of space. Generating, in consequence, a constant time in which the activities are not related to a schedule. The extension to the residential space of the experience of the airport, as a meeting space, which contains in the same place different times superposed.

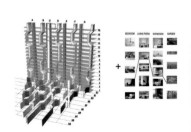

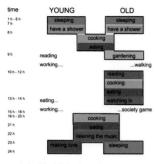

analysis of the individual and collective activitie

The self-sufficient city responds to the currewnt heterogeneous society a continuous flow of all types of people (age, culture, social class, religion) that gather in a same place but in a relative time. This concept focuses on the social sustainability, covering the demands and allowing the interaction of the user in the urban development. Atomized domestic uses: the dwelling as an addition of spaces spread through a structure, tied to a specific infrastructure and trajectory.

Non-Stop Dwelling:
- Customized catalogue chosen dwellings
- Atomized domestic uses
- Multifunctional shared spaces
- Sedentary and nomad lifestyles

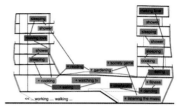

non-stop activities

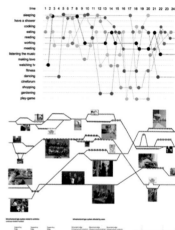

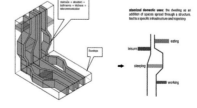

LIVING LANDSCAPES

URBAN GREEN

BIG INFRASTRUCTURES

ENERGY SYSTEMS

PARAMETRIC URBANISM

SOCIAL & COLLABORATIVE

THEORIES & STRATEGIES

RIGHT TO BE ITSELF (SUFFICIENT)

Solmi Laura

laura.solmi@student.unife.it

Italy

Urban areas expect to reach 2.000.000 population by 2030, despite of a rural population reduction.

To be active actors in this process we need to redescover the simple rules of the world's history.

HABITAT signifies HOME GROUND, that represents the unbreakable link between what is 'lived space' and what is 'livelble space'. This interaction supposes a BALANCE, and produces an INTERACTION that from an urban proiection means a relation between the major aspects of a community; environment, economy, policy and society.

This interaction determines the GENIUS LOCI, the place identity, the indissoluble bond between city and its site, that is evident in the small historic town, but not anymore in the big one.

To make it possible we should organise big cities into recognisable indipendent parts, safeguarding inside each ones its own identity.

By this way we can achieve an EVOLUTION based on an ORGANICAL GROWTH, that respects the different contributing aspects, following the principles of diversity, adaptability and flexibility.'

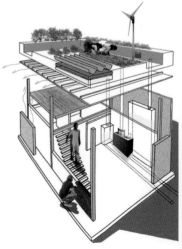

LIVING LANDSCAPES

URBAN GREEN

BIO INFRASTRUCTURES

ENERGY SYSTEMS

PARAMETRIC URBANISM

SOCIAL & COLLABORATIVE

THEORIES & STRATEGIES

SYMBIOTIC ENTITIES

Lee Tae Heung
Heyu Lu
leepab@gmail.com

Republic of Korea

Approximately between 9,000 to 10,000 years ago, civilization has begun along a number of river valleys throughout the southern half of Asia and Northern Africa for near rivers supplied an ample supply of water for agriculture and people's daily consumption. These rivers along with climate, vegetation, geography, and topography shaped the development of the early civilization. In addition to the development of civilization, the water supplies enabled the development of new technologies, economics, organizations, and innovations that which allowed the population to expand.

Water collection through the river and rain is gathered in a reservoir together. During this step, the portion of river water supplements essential minerals for the organism and vegetation while it mixes with the rain collection.

The collective water filters through the eco-system, which provides algae/moss growth for the fish to feed on.

The water fed to the aquaponics system creates a suitable atmosphere for the fish's growth along with their food. The fish's waste (fertilizer) is pumped through a compressor powered by PV cells into the hydroponics system.

Bypassing through the hydroponics system, the water is re-collected and stored in the water reservoir for further uses.

These propsed locations have crucial factor to be determined as the suitable potential locations for the sustainable buildings. Is it a considerably large city for social sustainability? Is it near the river bed or is accessible to water? Will percipitation affect the running of sustainable buildings?

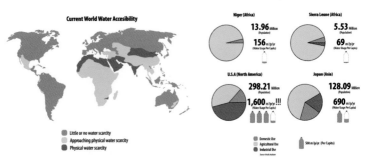

Current World Accesibility

Little or no water scarcity
Approaching physical water scarcity
Physical water scarcity

Niger (Africa)
13.96 Million (Population)
156 m³/p/yr (Water Usage Per Capita)

Sierra Leone (Africa)
5.53 Million (Population)
69 m³/p/yr (Water Usage Per Capita)

U.S.A (North America)
298.21 Million (Population)
1,600 m³/p/yr !!! (Water Usage Per Capita)

Japan (Asia)
128.09 Million (Population)
690 m³/p/yr (Water Usage Per Capita)

Domestic Use
Agricultural Use
Industrial Use

500 m³/p/yr (Per Capita)

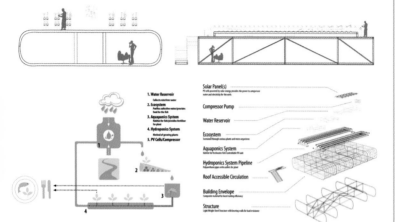

1. **Water Reservoir**
   Collects rainwater water
2. **Ecosystem**
   Purifies collective water/provides food for the fish
3. **Aquaponics System**
   Habitat for fish/provides fertilizer for plant
4. **Hydroponics System**
   Method of growing plants
5. **PV Cells/Compressor**

Solar Panel(s)
PV cells powered by solar energy provides the power to compressor water and electricity for the unit

Compressor Pump

Water Reservoir

Ecosystem
Sustained through various plants and micro organisms

Aquaponics System
Habitat for freshwater fish/controllable PV unit

Hydroponics System Pipeline
Polyurethane pipes with outlets for plant

Roof Accessible Circulation

Building Envelope
Composite material for least heating efficiency

Structure
Light Weight Steel Structure with bearing walls for load resistance

LIVING LANDSCAPES

URBAN GREEN

BIO-INFRASTRUCTURES

ENERGY SYSTEMS

PARAMETRIC URBANISM

SOCIAL & COLLABORATIVE

THEORIES & STRATEGIES

HURBS

WINNER

Sergio Castillo Tello
María Hernández Enríquez

mochi.studio@gmail.com

Spain

HURBS is a project aiming to reach the so often theorized sustainable urban environment through the development of adaptable design and participative tools.
–HURBS understands and addresses the city as a place where diverse and often contradictory interests meets. HURBS gets together parties that play a role in the complex urban system and allows them to work creatively in a sustainable collaboration.
–HURBS is an emergent and perfectible system, a participative interface assisting citizens shape the city. HURBS makes the most of already existing tools –i.e. the web – to help social participation customize the urban environment, making this process transparent.

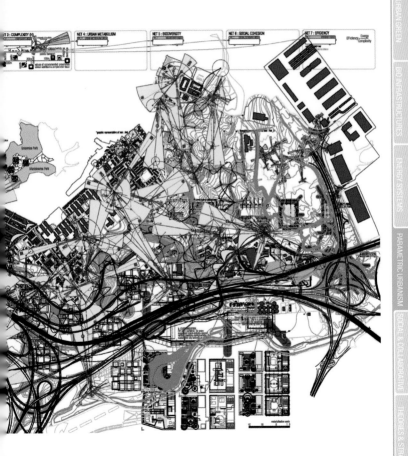

NET 3 : COMPLEXITY (H) NET 4 : URBAN METABOLISM NET 5 : BIODIVERSITY NET 6 : SOCIAL COHESION NET 7 : EFFICIENCY

LIVING LANDSCAPES

URBAN GREEN

BIO INFRASTRUCTURES

ENERGY SYSTEMS

PARAMETRIC URBANISM

SOCIAL & COLLABORATIVE

THEORIES & STRATEGIES

Sustainability

Is the capacity to endure. It can be defined in biological terms as the ability of an ecosystem to maintain ecological processes, functions, biodiversity and productivity into the future.

Collaboration

Is a recursive process where two or more people or organizations work together in an intersection of common goals — for example, an intellectual endeavor that is creative in nature—by sharing knowledge, learning and building consensus.

http://en.wikipedia.org/

Sustainable Collaboration

There are 3 main collaborators that will build the city

SPONSOR - the person or entity that will develop the selected site for the experiment. It can be public or private and his/her suggestion will lay the foundations of the new project.

RESOURCE EXPERT - The collaborator with ecological or sustainable knowlege, the one that will suggest specific solutions that will take into account the different studies and researches made after the *sponsor* made the new plan.

USER ON - SITE- The most important collaborator. The one that will eventually decide which is the best balance - solution combination to design the project, because this collaborator will base his/her opinion on real on-site experience so the project will not be made only with theorical decisions.

As a public experiment, the main tool for everyone interested on this project will be a website , with a simple interface that will show the process and development of the project on a real time plan, and a discussion forum in which all the differents opinions will be shown with their respective linked changes to the plan. Selfless help for sustainability, is decisive

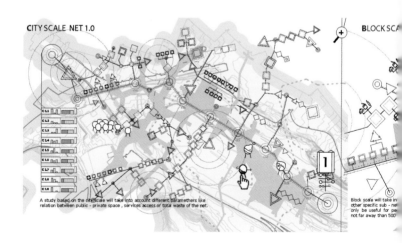

CITY SCALE NET 1.0

BLOCK SCA

A study based on the city scale will take into account different parameters like relation between public - private space , services access or total waste of the net.

Block scale will take in other specific sub - ne only be useful for pe not far than 500

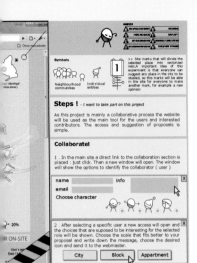

As a first approach, HURBS distinguishes 3 major players in the process of making a city:

The SPONSOR is the person or entity that develops any selected site. It is the public or private actor whose suggestions lay the foundations of the new scheme.

The RESOURCE EXPERT is a collaborator with ecological or sustainable knowledge who suggests specific solutions for the area to be developed taking into account different studies and researches.

The ON-SITE USER is the most important collaborator, and eventually decides the best solution to the area. His/her opinions -based on real on-site experience- avoid schemes that rely only on theoretical decisions.

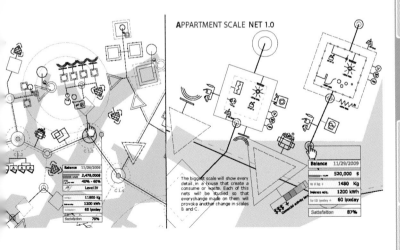

APPARTMENT SCALE NET 1.0

The biggest scale will show every detail in a house that create a consume or waste. Each of this nets will be studied so that everychange made on them will provoke another change in scales B and C.

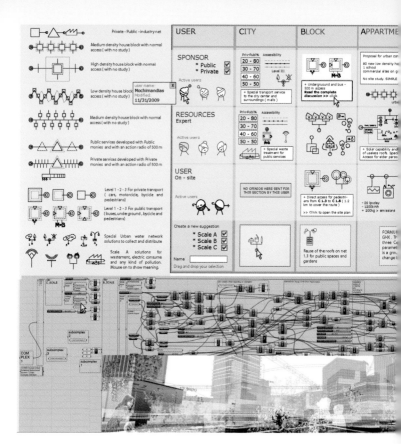

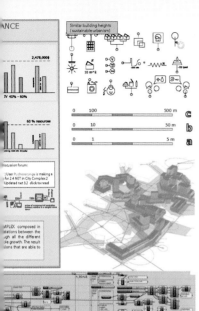

Similar building heights
(sustainable urbanism)

0	100	500 m	**c**
0	10	50 m	**b**
0	1	5 m	**a**

Any individual or group can be part of any and all parties and switch from one to another, therefore, the resulting interrelations between them and the development can be very complex. To simplify HURBS approach consists of three parts:

1. A comprehensive compilation of data –information & opinion- is gathered, analyzed and interrelated about any area of the city implementing a project. The data is orderly uploaded on a web page.

2. The web page -as an intuitive and accessible tool- allows citizens to participate, playing the role most suited to their interests. Every role is given many options and all of them are attached to programmed routines that affect and create urban patterns.

3. The materialization of the resulting project through HURBS uses Grasshopper™ as a graphical algorithm editor tightly integrated with Rhino's 3-D modeling tools. This parametric approach addresses all scales (city, block, apartment), and every network emerged after the previous steps.

HURBS aim is to develop a system in which cities result from their citizens' participation, not from economic or political interests that at one point were imposed as regulations.

ECO.NECTING

Vargas Diaz Ingrid Carolina
Eduardo Jimenez Morales

nurbarquitectos@yahoo.es

Colombia

Residential low density tissue represents 65% of the urban agglomeration growth of Granada-Spain. This uncontrolled occupation affects the environmental quality, network capacity and land value. It also increases urban sprawl and fragmentation. Our project is situated between those dispersed tissues and establishes a protocol of actions to guide their growth. The goals are the recovery of public space, the dissolution of ecological footprints and urban improvement. A re-thinking of conventional planning concepts: instead of a functional zoning, a hybrid uses pattern. Our proposal creates mobility junctions-like buildings, which contain accumulated program elements. It generates an ecological protective area to its surrounding. However, how can we preserve it? We decided to build it with primitive urban elements: a grid of native arboreal clusters which is able to restore identity to the territory. The result becomes an in-between public tissue to interweave the urban, rural and natural environment.

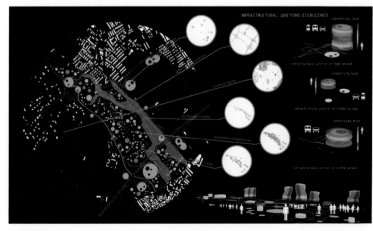

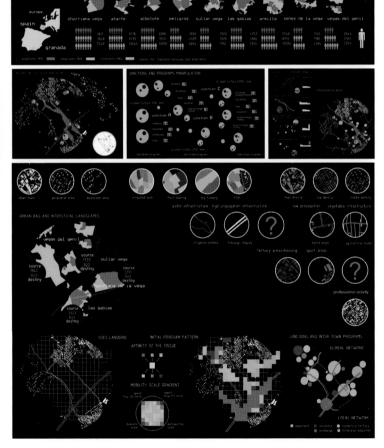

LIVING LANDSCAPES

URBAN GREEN

BIO-INFRASTRUCTURES

ENERGY SYSTEMS

PARAMETRIC URBANISM

SOCIAL & COLLABORATIVE

THEORIES & STRATEGIES

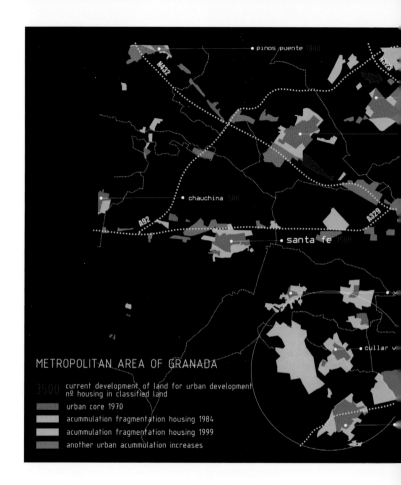

METROPOLITAN AREA OF GRANADA

3500 current development of land for urban development
nº housing in classified land

urban core 1970

acummulation fragmentation housing 1984

acummulation fragmentation housing 1999

another urban acummulation increases

pinos puente

chauchina

santa fe

cullar v

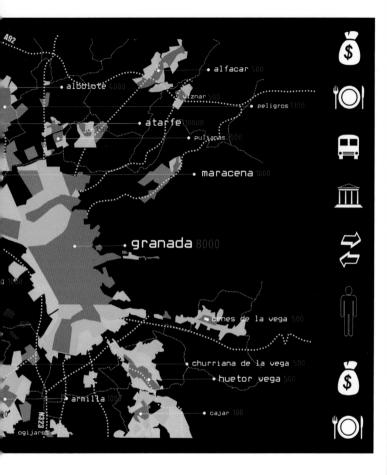

LIVING LANDSCAPES

URBAN GREEN

BIO INFRASTRUCTURES

ENERGY SYSTEMS

PARAMETRIC URBANISM

SOCIAL & COLLABORATIVE

THEORIES & STRATEGIES

PHOTOSYNTHESIS HEX-A-GONE

Kolev Hristomir
arch. Hristo Ivanov
office@x2studio.eu

Bulgaria

Chlorophyll. We took it as basis in the geometrical and functional development of the conception. Fundamental of existence. Idealistic example of renovation, new life, natural regenerator. We examined and drew inspiration from the graphical representation of the photosynthesis process.

From particular to general. From general to particular.

We used one general idea in modeling, positioning and zoning. We took advantage of the hexagonal module merits and subordinated the relations in the whole structure and its future development to this logic.

The hexagonal geometric system gave us more freedom in city planning in reference to world directions, sunlight, predominant winds and geodesic characteristics. This way all of the system's directions (infrastructure, buildings, planting, etc.) are with improved capabilities for development of directions – at intervals of 60° instead of 90°. Communications are realized by a local circular road, which may be transformed into an inner or a district ring-road.

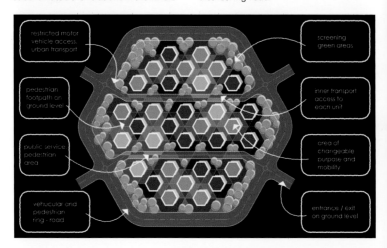

restricted motor vehicle access. urban transport

pedestrian footpath on ground level

public service pedestrian area

vehucular and pedestrian ring - road

screening green areas

inner transport access to each unit

area of changeable purpose and mobility

entrance / exit on ground level

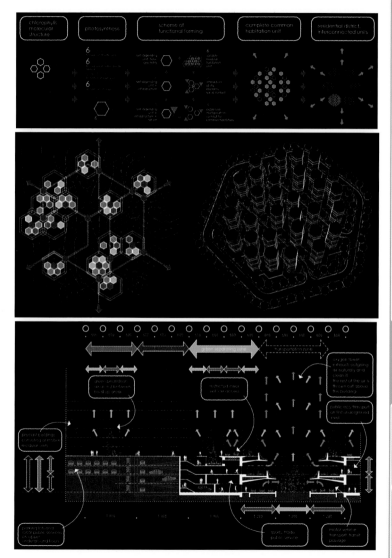

LIVING LANDSCAPES

URBAN GREEN

BIO INFRASTRUCTURES

ENERGY SYSTEMS

PARAMETRIC URBANISM

SOCIAL & COLLABORATIVE

THEORIES & STRATEGIES

DESERTIFICATION BARRIER

Ramady Ahmed
Ahmed El Basuony

otto_eng121@hotmail.com

Egypt

Dry projection

Provide that no circumstances were to change (though they will, and hardly for the best), all of Africa would be completely desertified by around the year 3800.faroff,it may seem ,but already within the next three or four generation, countries such as Senegal,Burkina Faso,Nigeria and Egyipt will face serious problems :they may even see their entire countries turn to desert.

Structure formation

Nomads using a simple ecological method which is some sort of "wicker trunks" as a barrier to be placed on the top of sand dunes trying to stop the movement of it and in case another dune is approaching they use an auxiliary row of the same plant.

From this point came the technique of the structure as a simulation to this ecological method.

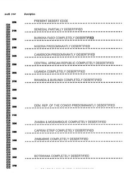

Sand dunes , Egypt

The roots stabilize the soil, the canopy shades the top soil which holds in the moisture for other plants to grow .

GROUND WATER
In the summer,comfortable internal temperature are maintained by pumping the ground water in to the tubes to a temperature of 45 degrees from a quite below the building via two specially drilled boreholes.the cold ground water is also used directly in the cooling coils of the air-handling units to cool the fresh air entering the building.the use of this natural resources for cooling reduces electricity consumption and thus saves money

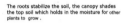
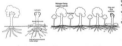

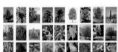

TUBES CONSTRUCTION: Rammed earth walls

step 1: framework is built and a layer of moist earth is filled in

step 2: the layer of moist earth is compressed

step 3: next layer of moist earth is added

step 4: successive layers of moist earth are added and compressed

step 5: remove the framework

step 6: the rammed earth wall

LIVING LANDSCAPES

URBAN GREEN

BIO INFRASTRUCTURES

ENERGY SYSTEMS

PARAMETRIC URBANISM

SOCIAL & COLLABORATIVE

THEORIES & STRATEGIES

Evolution phases

Year 00
To stop desertification The structure is a barrier to stop the movement of sand dunes and developing a thermal mass.

Year 05
According to geological studies Sand dunes is considered the biggest resource of ground water in the desert which can be extracted after a while of being stopped.
This water can be used for irrigation of some plants which roots stabilizes the soil while the canopy shades the top soil which holds in the moisture.

Year 10
Soil is now fertile and ready for agriculture and with that technique one day most of the desert will be like that.

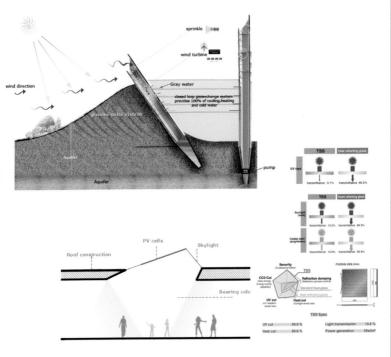

sprinkle

wind turbine

Gray water

closed loop geoexchange system provides 100% of cooling,heating and cold water

wind direction

passive solar system

Aquifer

Aquifer

pump

TSS		Heat reflecting glass	
UV rays			
	transmittance 0.1%		transmittance 40.5%

TSS		Heat reflecting glass	
Sunlight (heat)			
	transmittance 10.2%		transmittance 68.9%
Visible light (brightness)			
	transmittance 10.6%		transmittance 55.9%

Roof construction

PV cells

Skylight

Bearing colu

Security (shatterproof effect)

CO2 Cut (low-energy Energy-saving capability)

TSS

Reflection damping (Reflection pollution controls)

Standard float glass

Heat reflecting glass

UV cut (UV radiation shield ratio)

Heat cut (change shield ratio)

TSS Spec

module size (mm)

| UV cut | 99.8 % | Light transmission | 10.6 % |
| Heat cut | 89.8 % | Power generation | 42w/m² |

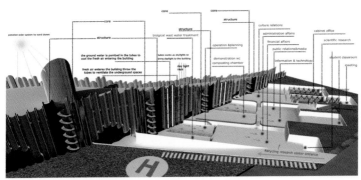

core

core

core

structure

structure

structure

culture relations

administration affairs

cabinet office

passive solar system by sand dunes

biological west water treatment

operation &planning

financial affairs

scientific research

the ground water is pumped in the tubes to cool the fresh air entering the building

tubes works as skylights to bring daylight to the building

demonstration wc composting chamber

public relations&media

student classroom

fresh air enters the building threw the tubes to ventilate the underground spaces

day light rock

information & technology

meeting

Recycling research center entrance

LIVING LANDSCAPES

URBAN GREEN

BIO INFRASTRUCTURES

ENERGY SYSTEMS

PARAMETRIC URBANISM

SOCIAL & COLLABORATIVE

THEORIES & STRATEGIES

URBAN AGRICULTURE

Jang Ryan
Sean Bailey
Anne Fougeron
Todd Aranaz

ryan@fougeron.com

United States

Imagine the city in 2108...
• By 2108, there will be 10 Billion peopl
in the world
• Yet in 2008, 80% of the land that is sui
able for raising crops is in use
• By the year 2050, nearly 80% of the
world's population will reside in urban
centers.
• How will we feed ourselves?

In 2108 San Francisco will stand as a
model sustainable city, where agricultu
is woven directly into the urban framework. Vertical agricultural systems, fec
by reclaimed water, and powered throu
renewable energy technologies, will be
deployed throughout the region.
— Through the appropriation of existing
structures, and the development of new
agricultural centers, along key nodes of
an area-wide transportation network, we
will begin to cultivate an urban environment that is linked directly to its food
supply.
— In this environment, food can be produced and distributed in a highly efficient
manner, eliminating the costly environmental effects of previous industrial
agricultural models, and providing a new
base of industry in an increasingly dense
and stratified urban environment.

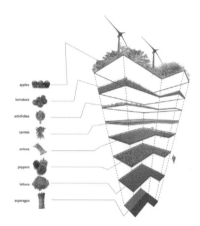

apples
tomatoes
artichokes
carrots
onions
peppers
lettuce
asparagus

LIVING LANDSCAPES

URBAN GREEN

BIO INFRASTRUCTURES

ENERGY SYSTEMS

PARAMETRIC URBANISM

SOCIAL & COLLABORATIVE

THEORIES & STRATEGIES

PHOTOVOLTAIC SKIN

DRIP IRRIGATION

WIND TURBINES

HOUSING UNIT

STORAGE UNIT

FOOD

[3] tier pier system

public
PEDESTRIAN
BICYCLE
URBAN GARDENSCAPE

monorail
BART EXTENSION

water treatment & utilities
GRAYWATER
BLACKWATER
UTILITIES

2019 2039 2099

EVOLUTION OF URBAN AGRICULTURE

LIVING LANDSCAPES

URBAN GREEN

BIO-INFRASTRUCTURES

ENERGY SYSTEMS

PARAMETRIC URBANISM

SOCIAL & COLLABORATIVE

THEORIES & STRATEGIES

CITY A & H

Segura Plaza Beatriz
Ignacio Perez Martinez
Silvia Noemi Segura Plaza

segura_arq@hotmail.com

Spain

With the benefit of hindsight, we have learnt that for a city to function self-sufficiently, a basic society which is capable of living independently is required. Therefore, the project begins with the creation of some principles and sociological changes which, when put into practice, will help to maintain the city of the 21st century. The project's priority is the creation of happy individuals, capable of continuous self-improvement; both individually and collectively; and who are able to meet the needs of the group as a whole. Alimentary self-sufficiency is proposed as an agreement between cities, where each develops itself according to its natural resources, and uses this advantage to develop relations between cultures, towns and neighbourhoods. From this, we create a model full of new concepts, which contribute to the evolution of the city; a city inhabited by social individuals who follow the rules of society. From this, we create a model full of new concepts, which contribute to the evolution of the city; a city inhabited by social individuals who follow the rules of society. 'Our society is based in a state of happiness and evolution which is achieved through maintaining a high level of curiosity, dynamism, innovation and participation between human beings.

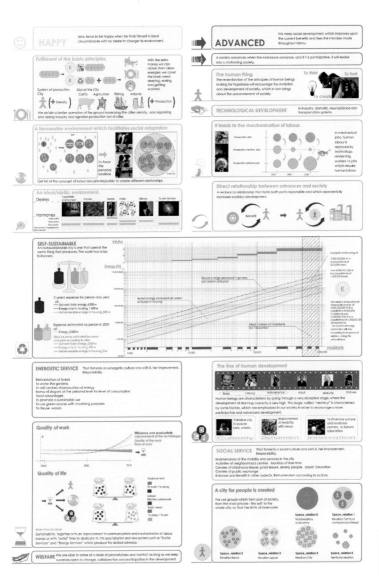

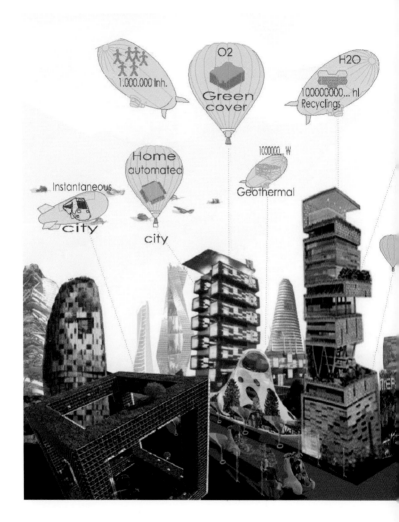

302

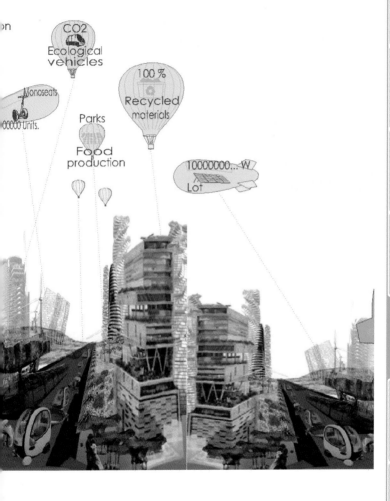

LIVING LANDSCAPES

URBAN GREEN

BIO INFRASTRUCTURES

ENERGY SYSTEMS

PARAMETRIC URBANISM

SOCIAL & COLLABORATIVE

THEORIES & STRATEGIES

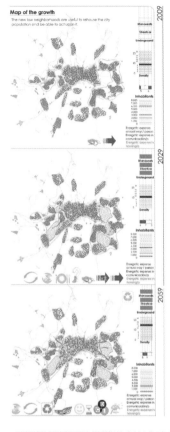

Map of the growth
The new low neighborhoods are useful to rehouse the city population and be able to act upon it.

2009

2029

2059

Facilitated by technological advances and social consciousness, it will allow people to develop themselves in the things that are intrinsically human; such as, thinking, creating, and feeling; as well as free-time to inhabit idyllic cities with environments which facilitate sociability and allow the fulfilment of the basic principles and respect towards Mother Earth'
Simplified in an elemental logic equation:

$$A \& H \rightarrow C \& B$$
H = Happiness
A = Advance and development
C = Attitude
B = Fulfilment of the basic principles

Although the model could be applied to a variety of different scales, we propose that the ideal scale would be a city with between 500,000 and 1 million inhabitants; that is to say a city where mobility is quick and efficient and covers a wide area, and at the same time has energetic green spaces on a human scale. The environment is capable not only of building a better relationship with nature, but creating areas of industry and food production, which can sustain the population with both produce and jobs.

Space_ relation 1
Proposed space of family residence or flat

3 students
Medicine-law
21-22-26 years old

3 person
parents + one son

2 personas
Couple pensioner
65-75 years old

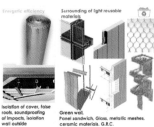

Energetic efficiency

Surrounding of light reusable materials

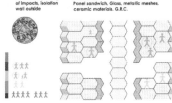

Isolation of cover, false roofs, soundproofing of impacts, isolation wall outside

Green wall, Panel sandwich, Glass, metallic meshes, ceramic materials. G.R.C.

Structural modular light system

Prefabricación, assembly and rapid disassembly

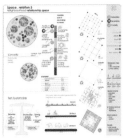

Space, relation 1
Neighbours relationship space

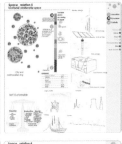

Space, relation 3
Territorial relationship space

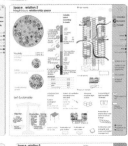

Space, relation 2
Neighbours relationship space

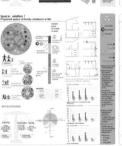

Space, relation 1
Proposed space of family residence or flat

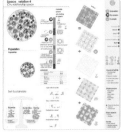

Space, relation 4
City relationship space

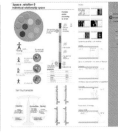

Space, relation 5
Individual relationship space

LIVING LANDSCAPES

URBAN GREEN

BIO INFRASTRUCTURES

ENERGY SYSTEMS

PARAMETRIC URBANISM

SOCIAL & COLLABORATIVE

THEORIES & STRATEGIES

H2O HELS.HYV.OULU - HELSINKI 2060

Philippon Alexandre
Albert Rolland
David Durand
Damien Peres
Sébastien Causse

tenozue@yahoo.fr

France

The purpose of this project was to imagine the future of the city of Helsinki and its suburbs in 2060. The project proposes to relocate the city area along an axis between North South linking the main Finnish cities. This axis is a particular infrastructure: the H^2 Automatic Highway. Based on the technological advanced of Finnish companies on the market of the communications and geographic coordinate systems, this infrastructure proposes to bring safely automobiles powered by hydrogen, allowing to consider a new design urban development as a transcontinental linear system. The second point developed by the project is a system of energy production based on the exploitation of the biomass through the Finnish wood industry: hydrogen is clean energy that could be used as fuel for future vehicles, which, once arrived at destination, would be transformed into generator, for example, to provide the energy necessary for a house.

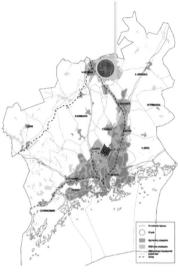

SEASON DIAGRAM

TERRITORY DIAGRAMS

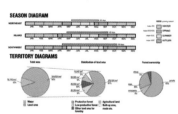

HYDROGEN & FUEL CELL DIAGRAMS

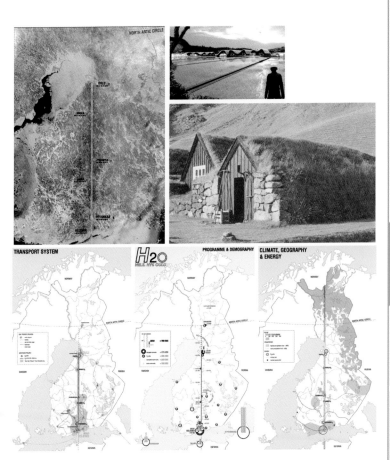

NORTH ARTIC CIRCLE

OULU

BRUCE

PEMBLLA

TYVARKAA

HELSINKI

TRANSPORT SYSTEM

H2O
HELL N°1 OULU

PROGRAMME & DEMOGRAPHY

CLIMATE, GEOGRAPHY & ENERGY

NORWAY

NORTH ARTIC CIRCLE

SWEDEN

RUSSIA

ESTONIA

LIVING LANDSCAPES

URBAN GREEN

BIO INFRASTRUCTURES

ENERGY SYSTEMS

PARAMETRIC URBANISM

SOCIAL & COLLABORATIVE

THEORIES & STRATEGIES

LIVING LANDSCAPES

URBAN GREEN

BIO INFRASTRUCTURES

ENERGY SYSTEMS

PARAMETRIC URBANISM

SOCIAL & COLLABORATIVE

THEORIES & STRATEGIES

CONTINU(C)ITY

Whitney Grant
Jassen Callender
Nick Hester
Bryan Norwood
wgrant@jcdc.caad.msstate.edu

United States

The American landscape is littered with 939 metro- and micropolitan statistical areas connected by 140,810 mile of rail and 2,615,870 miles of paved road. Overburdened lines of movement that serve to territorialize metropolitan areas. Cities and the transit between them have long been considered two elements functioning separately, but what happens when they take on the same identity? Continu(c)ity provides a way to reform cities and transit into a symbiotic, non-hierarchical, relationship. It is not the number of developments, population density, number of cars, miles of interstate, or sprawl that is the disease. These are symptoms of a more basic crisis: the organization of the body's organs—the failed relationship between metropolis and continental infrastructure. Continu(C)ity is a mile wide band of high density traversing the landscape defined by transit corridors on either side making movement more efficient, freeing up farmland, preserving biodiversity, and providing a more sustainable living environment.

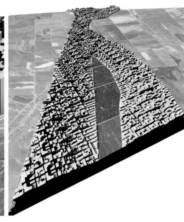

LIVING LANDSCAPES

URBAN GREEN

BIO INFRASTRUCTURES

ENERGY SYSTEMS

PARAMETRIC URBANISM

SOCIAL & COLLABORATIVE

THEORIES & STRATEGIES

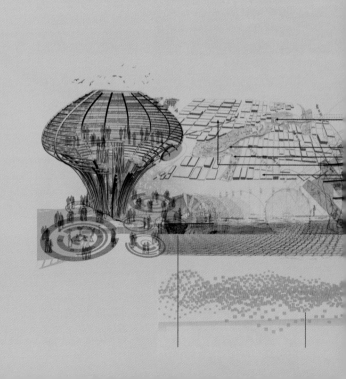

SOCIAL & CO-LLABO-RATIVE

LIVING LANDSCAPES

URBAN GREEN

BIO INFRASTRUCTURES

ENERGY SYSTEMS

PARAMETRIC URBANISM

SOCIAL & COLLABORATIVE

THEORIES & STRATEGIES

SOCIAL & COLLABORATIVE

The construction of a city starts with the
addition of layers. It is the consolidation of
phenomena, exchanges and activities that
combined to give rise to what we now know
as cities (a repetitive and perhaps obsolete term), and the principal agents of this
exchange have been human beings and their
relations with one another, through the flow
of matter, energy and information.
The city is the result of the addition of a variety of processes — formal, informal, emergent, planned and unplanned — involving
billions of people down through generations.
The elements of power are a direct reflection of self-organization within societies, and
have had a more than important role in the
morphological and phenomenological definition of those societies, now,
as we face a paradigm shift in terms of
power and the formal production of reality,
with the old 'top down' processes in crisis,
communities are no longer organizing themselves around centres of power but

in a distributed that is still in search of definition… communication makes the circulation of information more fluid and emergent processes have an ever greater influence on the production of reality: of course they always have done, but they are more evident now than ever.

We are experiencing a substantive change in the ways in which we interact, produce, and organize ourselves: the time has come for societies to organize themselves consciously, with the right tools, with clear objectives. It may be that we are lacking proposals for how to do this, for what do with so much technology, social networks, mobile devices and P2P; maybe we need ideas and applications that will enable us to handle emergent production so that we can arrive at a more optimal and efficient way of inhabiting our cities and of managing how we relate to one another.

Is the city a 'creatable' phenomenon? Can we decide to make a city as is a building?

LIVING LANDSCAPES

URBAN GREEN

BIG INFRASTRUCTURES

ENERGY SYSTEMS

PARAMETRIC URBANISM

SOCIAL & COLLABORATIVE

THEORIES & STRATEGIES

FINALIST

DRIFT CITY
A CONTINENTAL
TRANSIENT
INFRASTRUCTURE

Mc Dowell Andrew

smcdowell@lsu.edu

United States

Drift City is the hybridization of city and transportation at a continental scale. Rather than vastly separating highway from rail and industry from market Drift City imagines them as parallel entities. This extreme redundancy allows the drifter to continuously mediate between the two modes of transportation and production. Home is merged with the road and the rail. The concept involves the occupation of circulation so that the street, the stair and the landing become the framework for the home, the market and the factory. Conceived as a linear city similar to Le Corbusier's Plan for Algier's or Roger Chambless' Roadtown, the Highway city attempts to condense all aspects of a production oriented society into one strip of infrastructure.

Drift City is an urban strategy that responds to an unemployment crisis. It is an infrastructural city for a mobilized, nomadic, working society.

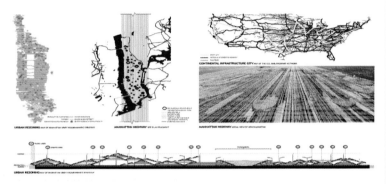

URBAN REZONING *map of occupation drift fragmentary strategy*

MANHATTAN HIGHWAY *site plan fragment*

CONTINENTAL INFRASTRUCTURE CITY *map of the U.S. railfreight network*

MANHATTAN HIGHWAY *aerial view of new condition*

URBAN REZONING *map of occupation drift fragmentary strategy*

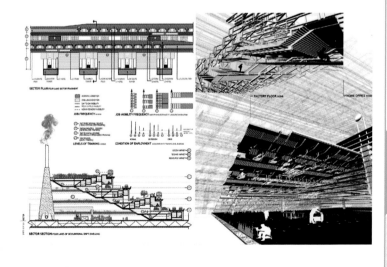

SECTOR PLAN *four lane sector fragment*

JOB FREQUENCY *scale*

JOB MOBILITY FREQUENCY *administered to the occupational zoning*

LEVELS OF TRAINING *scale*

CONDITION OF EMPLOYMENT *occupation training level subtext*

SECTOR SECTION *four lanes of occupational drift dwelling*

FACTORY FLOOR *scale*

HOME OFFICE *scale*

LIVING LANDSCAPES

URBAN GREEN

BIO INFRASTRUCTURES

ENERGY SYSTEMS

PARAMETRIC URBANISM

SOCIAL & COLLABORATIVE

THEORIES & STRATEGIES

SECTION A THE DEPOT SCENE

LIVING LANDSCAPES

URBAN GREEN

BIO INFRASTRUCTURES

ENERGY SYSTEMS

PARAMETRIC URBANISM

SOCIAL & COLLABORATIVE

THEORIES & STRATEGIES

H2090

FINALIST

Ponce Javier

archjjfp@yahoo.es

Spain

H2090, La Limonada , Guatemala city

" There is an estimate of 60,000 - 100.000 people living in "La Limonada". This is an urban slum community built into a ravine. It was stablished in the late 1950's by people who fled other areas of the country from various reasons"

Lemonade International

The proposal, presented in the competition under the motto "h2090", is inspired by the people in third world countries which are caught in a cycle of poverty without viable options of sustainable living. This futuristic scheme is based on hydrogen energy for XXI century self suf-

ficient neighborhoods. It aims to deal with the lack of social housing projects and became a model to follow

h2090 Masterplan main goals:

— Clean energy for the future (Hydrogen domestic net)

— Apply first world technology to third world countries

— Connect city areas through pedestrian eco-corridors

— Regenerate the existing urban fabric

— Recycle exisiting slum materials

— Organized environment where people can control/share their energy use

— encourage social interaction between social classes

— On site removable energies

— Gullies to become agri-parks

View of Guatemala´s Lemonade slum dividing 2 city zones

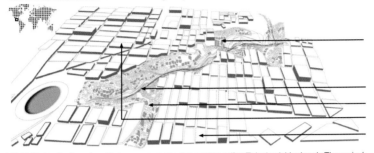

h2090 Masterplan based on Hydrogen energy for XXI century self sufficient neighborhoods. The project propose changes for an existing city which can be a model to follow for many third world countries

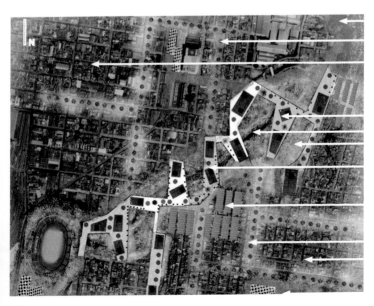

LIVING LANDSCAPES

URBAN GREEN

BIO INFRASTRUCTURES

ENERGY SYSTEMS

PARAMETRIC URBANISM

SOCIAL & COLLABORATIVE

THEORIES & STRATEGIES

LIVING LANDSCAPES

URBAN GREEN

BIO-INFRASTRUCTURES

ENERGY SYSTEMS

PARAMETRIC URBANISM

SOCIAL & COLLABORATIVE

THEORIES & STRATEGIES

SPACE AND LIES

Reynolds Benjamin John
Valle Medina

benreynolds4@hotmail.com

Australia

Industrial = Imposition
Give everyone the key to the city.
A tall skyscraper leaves a long shadow
(economy). Ironic transparent windows
spell an agenda-less architecture (and the
poignancy of an architectural year zero).

Submissions by the Public

Residents would vote for what design
represents a cause/style/future they
need. C'est possible: on fabrique, on
vend, on se paie (It is possible: we make
them, we sell them, we pay ourselves!)!

The Plug-less City

Exploit residues not voids (details).
Plug-In City? The (plug) is the message:

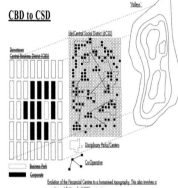

CBD to CSD

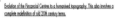

Evolution of the Financial Centres to a humanised topography. This also involves a
complete redefinition of old 20th century terms.

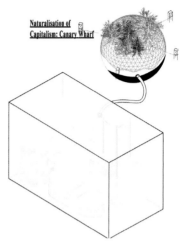

Naturalisation of Capitalism: Canary Wharf

a dramatis personæ. When we plug-in to something, for example land, we don't just obtain the resources to cook our food or water our garden, we plug-in to a whole history of (re-)written laws, drawn and ger- rymandered political demarcations, virgin- to-industrialised-to-sprawled-up-on earth. Thus these 'plugs' are the connections to a preprogrammed way of living mediated by private and governmental entities.
The Internet is the new CBD.
Dissolution = Resolution
Non-sensical buildings as National Banks would be now revamped by the masses as open plazas.
We will Never be Sustainable.
Property, Responsibility, Prothesis at Home.
De-formalisation of space.
Citizenship and Nationality..

Horizontality and the Internet

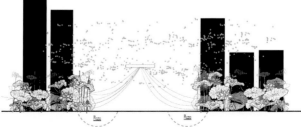

LIVING LANDSCAPES

URBAN GREEN

BIO INFRASTRUCTURES

ENERGY SYSTEMS

PARAMETRIC URBANISM

SOCIAL & COLLABORATIVE

THEORIES & STRATEGIES

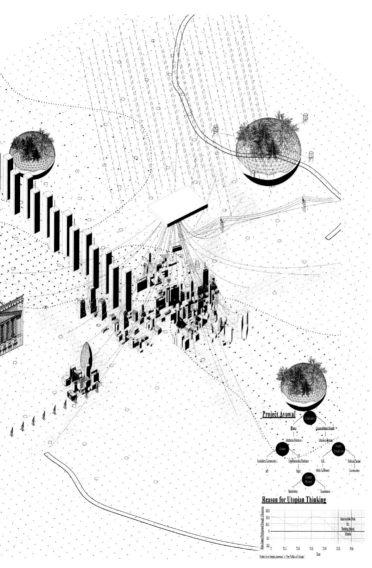

LIVING LANDSCAPES

URBAN GREEN

BIO INFRASTRUCTURES

ENERGY SYSTEMS

PARAMETRIC URBANISM

SOCIAL & COLLABORATIVE

THEORIES & STRATEGIES

Project Avowal

Reason for Utopian Thinking

SOCIOECOLOGICAL-TREES

Alonso Villodre Rubén

alvillo3@hotmail.com

Spain

Indicator
The indicator understands each other as a method to guarantee the effectiveness and objectives of the project: sostenibility + sociability + quality of life.

Artificial nature
An arboreal architecture doesn't only like an image, it's a relationship nexus.

Biodiversity
Basing us on the texts of AEMA, the project incorporates the biodiversity like a sustainable aspect.

Location
The project will be located in Tenerife's island, Spain, concretely in a tourist complex that is being obsolete (in favour of affable encounters).

Green leisure
The characteristic leisure of these places is looked for to generate a public conscience with an international character.

7 natural ecosystems
Recreation of the seven ecosystems in Tenerife in the level 1 of the object (top).

Public consciousness
It seeks to become aware to the society of the biodiversity through the leisure and performance.

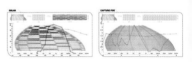

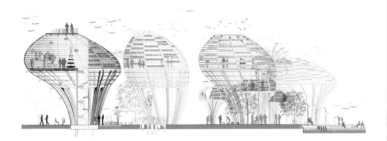

LIVING LANDSCAPES

URBAN GREEN

BIO INFRASTRUCTURES

ENERGY SYSTEMS

PARAMETRIC URBANISM

SOCIAL & COLLABORATIVE

THEORIES & STRATEGIES

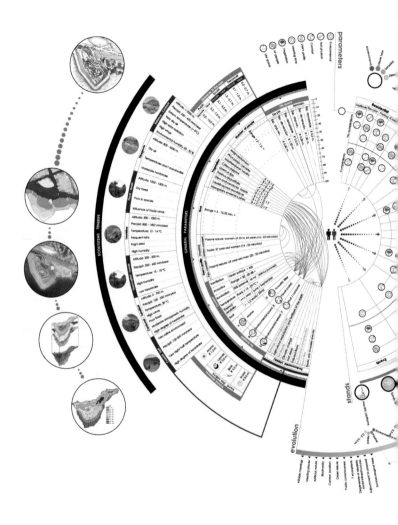

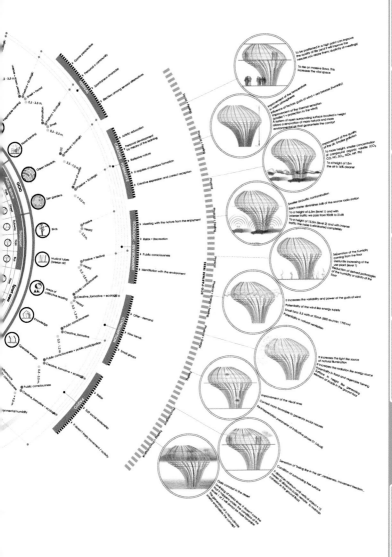

LIVING LANDSCAPES

URBAN GREEN

BIO INFRASTRUCTURES

ENERGY SYSTEMS

PARAMETRIC URBANISM

SOCIAL & COLLABORATIVE

THEORIES & STRATEGIES

SWARM CITY

Winnie Carola
Prem Balasubramanian

carola.winnie@gmail.com

India

Adyar is a large neighbourhood in south Chennai (formerly Madras), Tamil Nadu, India. It is located on the southern banks of the Adyar River. It is partly a representation of the city of Chennai itself.

Yesterday and Today- Snippets from the Media

How urbanisation watered down the natural wealth

Chennai and its suburbs once boasted of over 100 small and big water bodies. A majority of them have been gradually destroyed due to a combination of hectic urbanisation and anthropogenic interferences.

Death of an estuary

The Adyar estuary is a textbook case of a fragile natural heritage losing out to frenzied urbanisation, a process that has happened in many cities.

Tomorrow

The Proposal: The year is 2065 AD. Building the Self- Sufficient System happens at three levels:

THE CELL
Cell Systems:

The cell is designed as a polymer resin light weight structure that it can suspend itself in air with the help of carbon- nanotubes which inturn are fragments of a larger energy source.

THE ORGAN
The Pod:

The pod is a charged electric plate which is suspened in air by creating an energy field. It can float in air without physical support by the phenomenon of Electrostatic induction

Air Terrains:

Each cell is equipped with an intelligent system which is programmed to direct wind in a particular manner according to the climate belt that the cell is situated in.

THE BODY
The SWARM CITY is a completely balanced system where every form of energy consumption is recycled and used.

Why should a city float?

a) No more digging of foundations.

b) Soil quality is not depleted.

c) Ground water is replenished

d) Efficient waste management systems promotes efficient re-use

e) The produce of farming and orchards by the river can sustain the 'floating' community above it.

f) Where humidity is high, air terrains optimise wind flow and maintain ambient environments.

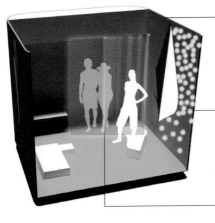

The skin of the cell is made of polymer resin fibres ...

The skin aquires electricity from the carbon nanotube by which each cell is suspened.

Carbon nano screens can produce holographic images .

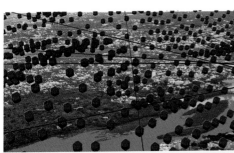

CHENNAI BLUE-GREEN PATCH

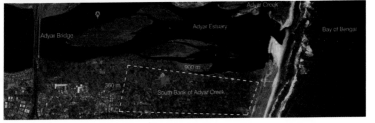

Adyar Creek

Adyar Estuary

Bay of Bengal

Adyar Bridge

900 m

360 m

South Bank of Adyar Creek

LIVING LANDSCAPES

URBAN GREEN

BIO INFRASTRUCTURES

ENERGY SYSTEMS

PARAMETRIC URBANISM

SOCIAL & COLLABORATIVE

THEORIES & STRATEGIES

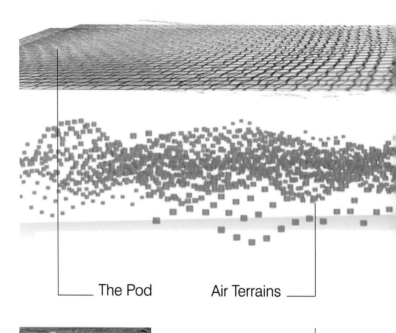

The Pod   Air Terrains

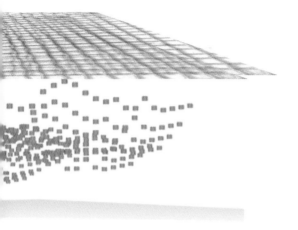

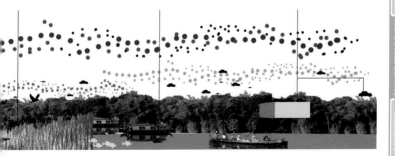

LIVING LANDSCAPES

URBAN GREEN

BIO INFRASTRUCTURES

ENERGY SYSTEMS

PARAMETRIC URBANISM

SOCIAL & COLLABORATIVE

THEORIES & STRATEGIES

CSW

Campos Carlos Daniel
Arq. Yamila Zynda Aiub
Colaboradores:
Pedro Magnasco
Ignacio Savid
Ignacio Boscolo
ccamposarq@yahoo.com

Argentina

Living among sounds
Noise can be also a renewable source of energy.
Cities are noisy environments.
Day & Night, Soundscapes are gradual processes we are immerse in
Like a storm, traffic jam, a school lunch break, a dog's bark.
Our cities express themselves as the sound of their space.
This proposal pursues the possibility of creating a new city, into our city, by the re-organization of sound and noise, and the creation of new soundscapes.
Each time a building is under construction, a lot of aggressive noises invade the city.

The soft-spongy condition of CSW Fabric will absorb noise and collect energy out of this process. A noise-trap.
Street Traffic lines painted with CSW sound-absorbent painting, Urban facilities covered with CSW fabric, free plot CSW temporary occupiers, CSW urban benches, fences, gates and sound absorbent working clothes.
What is a CSW unit?
A CSW Unit is a spatial module, a blue translucent bubble connectable as a cube. The origin is the path of QUAD, by Samuel Beckett, an endless promenade involving sides and diagonals of a square. A CSW unit is a QUAD promenade in space, into the form of a cube, instead of a square.

2 units

4 units

16 units

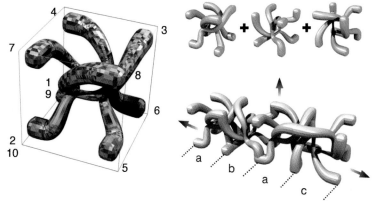

LIVING LANDSCAPES

URBAN GREEN

BIO-INFRASTRUCTURES

ENERGY SYSTEMS

PARAMETRIC URBANISM

SOCIAL & COLLABORATIVE

THEORIES & STRATEGIES

LIVING LANDSCAPES

URBAN GREEN

BIO INFRASTRUCTURES

ENERGY SYSTEMS

PARAMETRIC URBANISM

SOCIAL & COLLABORATIVE

THEORIES & STRATEGIES

RECIPROCITY

Jason Butz
Carla Landa
Francis D'Andrea
Martha Skinner

jbutz@clemson.edu

United States

Envisioned as a self-sustaining community Reciprocity can either serve as the foundation for a new city, or as an intervention in current cities. Reciprocity intends to take what waste its inhabitants produce and use it in alternative ways before it is ultimately turned into a recyclable state. Waste that would otherwise be diverted to landfills is used to construct each pod. As new habits form disposing of waste is no longer a hassle, instead it is a way of life. Just as the waste is used temporarily for some greater purpose, the clusters as a whole facilitate temporary resuscitators of a city in peril. Imagine a waterfront city ravaged by a storm. Reciprocity is dispatched in masses and the destruction becomes fuel while the pods serve as temporary displaced housing units. A symbiotic relationship is created and a flexible network begins to bridge the gaps in the cycles we helped to break.

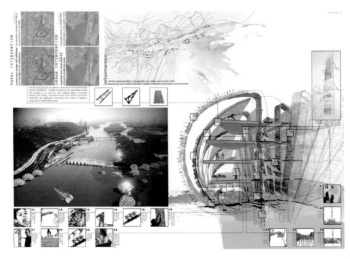

LIVING LANDSCAPES

URBAN GREEN

BIO INFRASTRUCTURES

ENERGY SYSTEMS

PARAMETRIC URBANISM

SOCIAL & COLLABORATIVE

THEORIES & STRATEGIES

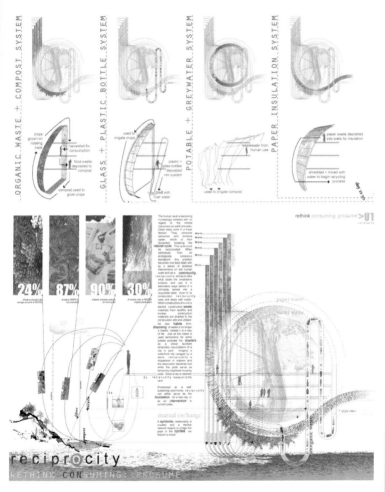

ORGANIC WASTE + COMPOST SYSTEM

crops grown on rotating track

harvested for consumption

food waste deposited to compost

compost used to grow crops

GLASS + PLASTIC BOTTLE SYSTEM

used to irrigate crops

plastic + glass bottles deposited into system

planter with river water

POTABLE + GREYWATER SYSTEM

wastewater from human use

used to irrigate compost

PAPER INSULATION SYSTEM

paper waste deposited into walls for insulation

shredded + mixed with water to begin recycling process

rethink consuming prosume >01

24% 87% 90% 30%

mutual exchange

reciprocity

RETHINK CONSUMING: PROSUME

paper waste

water waste

organic waste

341

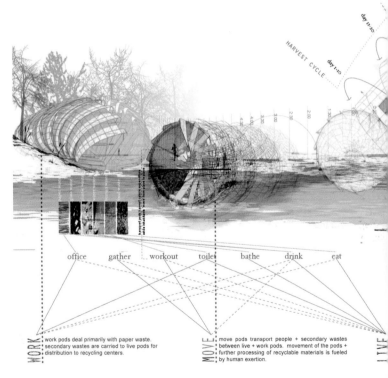

HARVEST CYCLE

day 11-20

day 1-10

4:00
3:00
2:00
1:00

transport pods harvest cubic square meters
while inhabitants move from place to place

office   gather   workout   toilet   bathe   drink   eat

WORK : work pods deal primarily with paper waste. secondary wastes are carried to live pods for distribution to recycling centers.

MOVE : move pods transport people + secondary wastes between live + work pods. movement of the pods + further processing of recyclable materials is fueled by human exertion.

LIVE

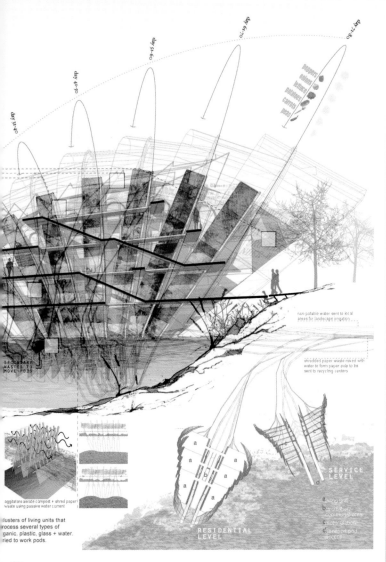

LIVING LANDSCAPES

URBAN GREEN

BIO INFRASTRUCTURES

ENERGY SYSTEMS

PARAMETRIC URBANISM

SOCIAL & COLLABORATIVE

THEORIES & STRATEGIES

day 11-40
day 41-50
day 51-60
day 61-70
day 71-80

papers
cables
lettuce
rubbers
carrots
peas

non-potable water sent to local
areas for landscape irrigation

shredded paper waste mixed with
water to form paper pulp to be
sent to recycling centers

SECONDARY
WASTES TO
MOVE PODS

aggitators aerate compost + shred paper
waste using passive water current

...lusters of living units that
...rocess several types of
...ganic, plastic, glass + water.
...ried to work pods.

SERVICE
LEVEL

a living unit
b circulation
common areas
c work pods
d transport pod
access

RESIDENTIAL
LEVEL

343

FREEDOM IN CAPTIVITY

Casali Duccio

cioduc@hotmail.com

Italy

All human beings on the planet live concentrated within the same city, wich is a huge megalopolis under a dome...
Outside the dome nature take its natural course of evolution, undisturbed, the plants and animals thrive freely, untouched, far from any contact with humans...
Freedom in Captivity
Our plan contemplates the merger of the entire human population within a single huge metropoly organized and urbanistically planned for ensuring every individual the living space needed and any kind of service.
The first objective of this project is to safeguard from an ecological point of view the planet earth.
We believe that concentrating the human population within a unique complex designed and planned to welcome it in its entirety, it is possible to enable the land to regain its natural life process.

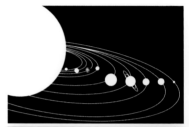

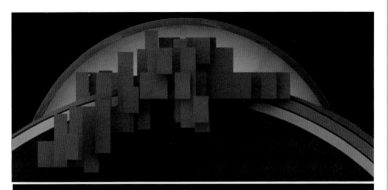

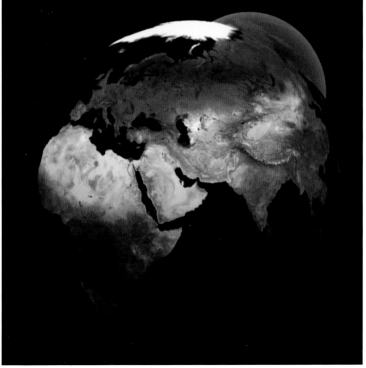

LIVING LANDSCAPES
URBAN GREEN
BIG INFRASTRUCTURES
ENERGY SYSTEMS
PARAMETRIC URBANISM
SOCIAL & COLLABORATIVE
THEORIES & STRATEGIES

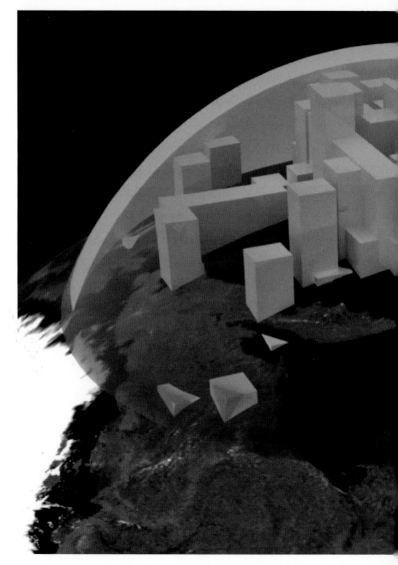

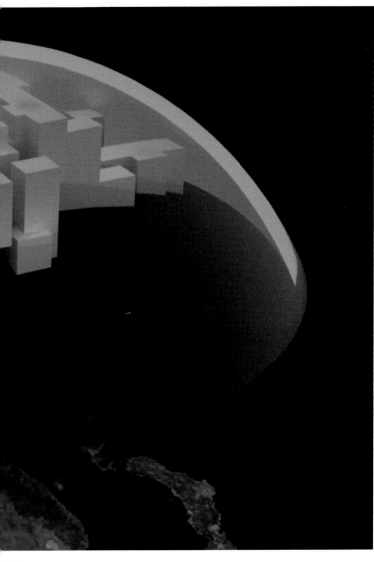

LIVING LANDSCAPES

URBAN GREEN

BIO-INFRASTRUCTURES

ENERGY SYSTEMS

PARAMETRIC URBANISM

SOCIAL & COLLABORATIVE

THEORIES & STRATEGIES

EVOLVING URBANITY

Allaix Francesco

francesco.allaix@gmail.com

Italy

The habitat of the XXI century cannot be planned. As Louis Kahn said, "If you know how something will be in 50 years, you can do it now. But you don't know it, because the aspect of something in 50 years will be as it will be".

What it is possible to provide, though, is an open strategy, a backbone flexible enough to manage urban evolution.

Three tools essential to this strategy:
- close the loops to achieve self-sufficiency, like in the flow of renewable energy, changing of functions within the building or recycling of materials;
- develop both high-tech, engineering solutions (sustainable production and use of energy) and low-tech, architectural solutions (sustainable design and use of the built environment);
- take in account both stable and instable elements to adapt to internal and external variables from the very beginning.

This case study is on Kalasatama, Helsinki's former eastern harbour.

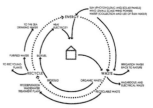

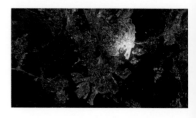

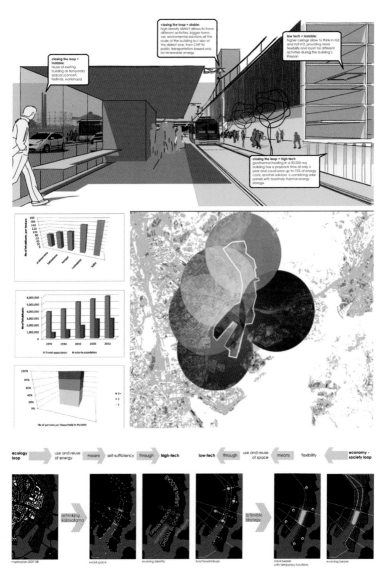

LIVING LANDSCAPES

URBAN GREEN

BIO INFRASTRUCTURES

ENERGY SYSTEMS

PARAMETRIC URBANISM

SOCIAL & COLLABORATIVE

THEORIES & STRATEGIES

closing the loop + instable:
reuse of existing building as temporary spaces (concert, festivals, workshops)

closing the loop + stable:
high density district allows to have different activities, bigger turnover, environmental solutions at the scale of the building but also at the district one, from CHP to public transportation based only on renewable energy

low tech + instable:
higher ceilings allow to think in m3 and not m2, providing more flexibility and room for different activities during the building's lifespan

closing the loop + high tech
geothermal heating in a 30.000 m.q. building has a payback time of only 4 year and could save up to 75% of energy costs; another solution is combining solar panels with borehole thermal energy storage

ecology loop → use and reuse of energy → meant → self-sufficiency → through → high-tech ← low-tech ← through ← use and reuse of space ← means ← flexibility ← economy - society loop

masterplan 2007-08 → rethinking kalasatama → social space → evolving identity → functional linkups → a flexible strategy → initial bearer with temporary functions → evolving bearer

URBAN BLOCKS

349

ZMVM

Cesar Katia
Hugo Vargas Rosales
architektenhv@gmail.com

Mexico

The principal and most important is the excesive use of water, due the extraction percentaje, exceeds the recharge. the aquifers of the zmvm are over exploited,due the growing demand.the zmvm has 13 rivers, that are used to evacuate the wasted water that the city produce. the hidden rivers are mixcoac, churubusco, piedad and consulado, this also are part of the most important avenues that connects the city, and exist nine more that are open, but they are also used for wasted water.due the climate changes the world has been suffering with the global warm, the climate has been modified, to extreme, this has been harmed to the zmvm, with stormy rains that has affected the open rivers that

contains wasted water,delivering with the overflow affecting the borders zones.
water disaster
from the analysis of the zmvm the motion for sustainable city borns since existing problems with the water. to start from urban recycling the river could be used as central axis of ecotechnology. the rivers to used are viaducto, churubusco, piedad, mixcoac and consulado, this are the elements that distribute not only water but also, build up a green shelter that wil have out doors improving the public space. the river will have treatment plants, also will be used as a storage of rain water, this will reduce the water consumption.

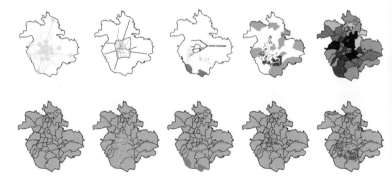

LIVING LANDSCAPES

URBAN GREEN

BIO INFRASTRUCTURES

ENERGY SYSTEMS

PARAMETRIC URBANISM

SOCIAL & COLLABORATIVE

THEORIES & STRATEGIES

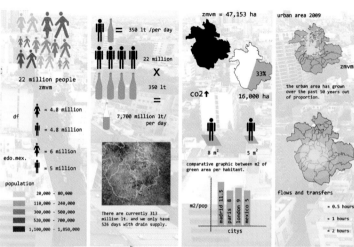

22 million people
zmvm

df

= 4.8 million

= 4.8 million

edo.mex.

= 6 million

= 5 million

population

20,000 - 80,000
110,000 - 240,000
300,000 - 500,000
520,000 - 700,000
1,100,000 - 1,850,000

= 350 lt /per day

22 million

X

350 lt

=

7,700 million lt/
per day

There are currently 313
million lt. and we only have
526 days with drain supply.

zmvm = 47,153 ha

urban area 2009

co2↑

33%

16,000 ha

8 m²   5 m²

comparative graphic between m2 of
green area per habitant.

m2/pop

madrid 11.5
paris 8
london 9
mexico 5

citys

the urban area has grown
over the past 50 years out
of proportion.

zmvm

flows and transfers

= 0.5 hours
= 1 hours
= 2 hours

water treatment

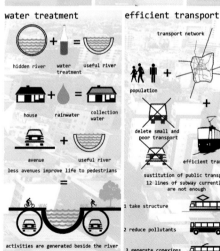

hidden river   water treatment   useful river

house   rainwater   collection water

avenue   useful river

less avenues improve life to pedestrians

=

activities are generated beside the river

urban regenerationof a river that now
is hidden and belongs to an important
avenue becoming the central axis of a
sustainable approach.

efficient transport

transport network

population

delete small and
poor transport

efficient transport

sustitution of public transport
12 lines of subway currently
are not enough

1 take structure

2 reduce pollutants

3 generate conexions

is necessary for getting around the city
efficient transportation and quality in
the service.

sustainable

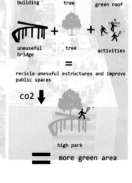

building   vegetation   green wall

building   tree   green roof

uneuseful bridge   tree   activities

=

recicle unsuful estructures and improve
public spaces

co2 ↓

high park

more green area

THIRD BELGRADE

Grujevska Jovana
Draskovic Natasa
Medjo Zorica
Delibasic Milica

jovanagr@gmail.com

Serbia

Belgrade, the city on two rivers, city with three coasts, city on three cities. First Belgrade, the old city, the medieval one's city, city of carriage. Second Belgrade, the new city, the industrial one's city, city of machine. Third Belgrade? Still indefinited number three. Can it be the city of the healthy one?

Human, as the center of our interest, is defined through the unity of body, mind and soul, as parts of an unbreakable circle. As defined, a free person is realized in spaces that are balanced as well, where they are not a stranger, but where they control, direction and create themself their own worlds. A project that creates itself. The idea is to give just a starting impulse and direction its performance and to let a user of the space create and form said space, creating an identity of the region and a feeling of belonging to a certain place.

Sometimes the best reaction of an architect is to suppress themself from the construction, creating a necessary frame but leaving a user the possibility of enjoying the free space. Natural potential is the most important concern for defining the goal of the project. Conserving the advancement of this potential is

LIVING LANDSCAPES

URBAN GREEN

BIO INFRASTRUCTURES

ENERGY SYSTEMS

PARAMETRIC URBANISM

SOCIAL & COLLABORATIVE

THEORIES & STRATEGIES

accomplished by intervening, in the sense of introducing users who would use it in the right way, namely this way it is gained a large number of users in compared to precent of built structure, and a small number compared to area of unbuilt natural environment. This way, human of today, distanced from their real nature, comes back to feelings, perception, enjoying, through all three elements that build them.

Three paths (visual, audio, tactile) activate senses and lead him through ambients, where he would activate something that has been neglected in todays technological and computerized world, letting him choose his own path. Paths lead to the river and interconnect with it. The river represent a continuum, and not a finite limit. Communication and permeation, but peace. We intervened in two directions, creating of public spaces that are vibrant and free enough to encourage communication, and tolerant enough to leave silent retreats.

On the way from the residential area to the river, three paths lead them through spaces, in which they can enjoy or accidentally find silence, shade, a friend, a seducing look...

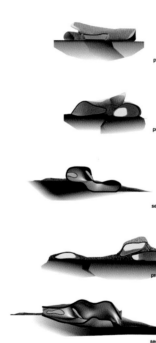

presek C C

presek A A

section A A

presek B B

section C C

section B B

LIVING LANDSCAPES

URBAN GREEN

BIO INFRASTRUCTURES

ENERGY SYSTEMS

PARAMETRIC URBANISM

SOCIAL & COLLABORATIVE

THEORIES & STRATEGIES

HYDROPONIC FARMERS MARKET

Leung Michael

leung.mkl@gmail.com

United States

In order to accommodate the increase of population in the San Francisco Bay Area the region will require a new infrastructure that can collect, distribute water, power, fuel, and good to accommodate the needs of residents and visitors. Through the exploration of environmental phenomena present in the Bay Area, this project investigates the notion of fog collection, urban agriculture, and distribution of farmed goods in the surrounding regions of San Francisco. The facility is comprised of a promenade at Ocean Beach, which serves to contain a volume of fog-condensing polypropylene meshes which result in water to be filtered and used as irrigation for a hydroponic farm. The plants are farmed in a vertical hydroponic system which uses a stacked pod modular unit for irrigation. The produce is then placed in storage areas for greater distribution to the San Francisco Region, as well as distributed in the farmers market loggia facing Golden Gate Park. Parametric logic was used to generate both the fog collection meshes, as well as the hydroponic vertical wall in order to provide an array of opening sizes. The design of both screen systems stems from studies of biomimetic principles, which is a result of learning from a precedent in nature.

Providing Food Sustainably

By looking at the life cycle and transportation of food in cities it is evident that bringing agriculture closer to neighborhoods allow for a more efficient and sustainable infrastructure. Combined with architectural interventions, this idea would become an urban revolution that looks

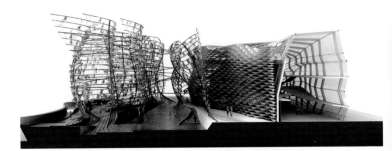

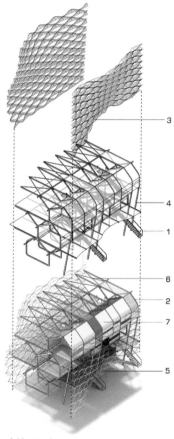

at city planning with a cultural attitude which is justified by economic, social, and environmental benefits. Locally grown produce serves to enhance these links as well as provide a community bond predicated on benefits of vitality resulting from community gardens, farmers markets, and city farms. The public nature of food bring people together in urban spaces where there are opportunities for casual interaction through buying, eating, and growing food, or planned interaction through dining and meeting at cafes. By eating within a particular region where the food is cultivated, it provides a distinct connection to place.

Construction Concept

The project deals with the sustainable development of a hydroponic farm, education center, and farmers market which attempts to foster a symbiotic relationship between urban and rural citizens by using productive landscapes as an interface for exchange. Each of the classroom units are embedded within a structure that is prefabricated and modularized, to allow for the hydroponic farm to be built up over time. The temporary habitation is akin to the ebbs and flows of the ocean waves at the threshold of the site.

1. Migrant worker entry
2. Metal panels/screen
3. Hydroponic component planter
4. Pre-fab structural steel members
5. Corian thermo-formed planter components
6. Lateral Support and trellis system for vines
7. Migrant farmer housing module

LIVING LANDSCAPES

URBAN GREEN

BIO INFRASTRUCTURES

ENERGY SYSTEMS

PARAMETRIC URBANISM

SOCIAL & COLLABORATIVE

THEORIES & STRATEGIES

Housing for the Migrant Community

1. Storage for farming facility
2. Metal grate flooring
3. Hydroponic component planter
4. Vertical circulation to hydroponics
5. Stainless steel pre-fab stacked fram
6. Lateral Support and trellis for vine plants
7. Migrant farmer housing module

FLOOR PLAN OF HOUSING UNIT

SECTION OF MIGRANT FARMER HOUSING

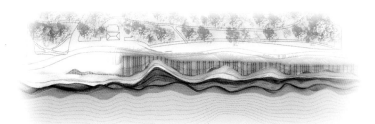

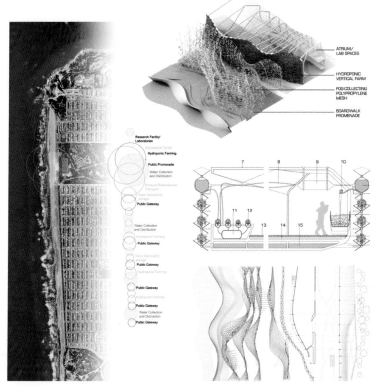

ATRIUM/
LAB SPACES

HYDROPONIC
VERTICAL FARM

FOG-COLLECTING
POLYPROPYLENE
MESH

BOARDWALK
PROMENADE

Research Facility/
Laboratories

Educational Center

Hydroponic Farming

Public Promenade

Water Collection
and Distribution

Produce/Pedestrian
Transport

Farm Harvesting
Storage

Public Gateway

Water Collection
and Distribution

Hydroponic Farming

Public Gateway

Farm Harvesting
Storage

Public Gateway

Hydroponic Farming

Public Gateway

Hydroponic Farming

Public Gateway

Water Collection
and Distribution

Public Gateway

LIVING LANDSCAPES

URBAN GREEN

BIO INFRASTRUCTURES

ENERGY SYSTEMS

PARAMETRIC URBANISM

SOCIAL & COLLABORATIVE

THEORIES & STRATEGIES

REPOWER CITY

Valdes Lenin

lev_letters@hotmail.com

Mexico

This project is much more than an urban programming, is not the answer to the bigger troubles about a city, it's in fact: an escape to the older concepts that emerge into the architectural language: space and form. The new challenges are looking for order, much more than identity, into the chaos; the challenges are looking for answers to start building equalization out the noise that deafens the sane growing of our daily life. Trough the "repowered city" and its concepts

The city is not the centre anymore, is not just the system explained by Karl Marx on his material-economical theories. At this moment the democracy is taking a new force, so, the governments must be prepared to take decisions in favor of the people.

The repowered city is a system proposed to normalize the city, going around the city and project new nodes with similar capabilities of integration of services, including places to rest, work and in the integral way is not urbanization but a programming with logic of humanity.

With this program we expect to amplify the development in places where people is not integrated to the city, repowering the diversity into them own skills and resources. At this way those de-concentrated places will be integrated not just as a regional hierarchy, or a concentrated centre. The proposal is to concentrate the solution around a balanced and sustainable development.

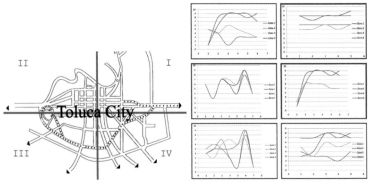

LIVING LANDSCAPES

URBAN GREEN

BIO INFRASTRUCTURES

ENERGY SYSTEMS

PARAMETRIC URBANISM

SOCIAL & COLLABORATIVE

THEORIES & STRATEGIES

RURBAN SETTLEMENT

Dudareva Liva

liva.dudareva@gmail.com

Latvia

The project is based on new urban design phenomenon Rurban Settlement that explores the relationship between eco-systems and information society in the teritories that have undergone a massive change and transformation. It becomes a live issue in the context of regeneration of disused urban and industrial territories today. The urban design idea lies in modu-larity and flexible and interactive applica-tion to abandoned industrial and derilicted lands in the borderlands that could be applied and adjusted worldwide.

Rurban Settlement becomes an interac-tive and inclusive planning tool - inter-face between people and their habitat. Degraded territories are developed in a cultural and recreational centres and new wildlife sanctuaries of the region.

Interface — *"Each surface is an interface between two environments that is ruled by constant activity in the form of an exchange between the two substances placed in contact with one another."*

P. Virilio "Lost Dimension"

Referring to what Paul Viriljo has said - what was periphery and border, becomes interface - an active interaction space. Thus Rurban settlement acquires principles of ecotone - a transition from one ecosystem into other: city becoming a countryside. Human habitat becomes ecosystem.

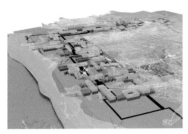

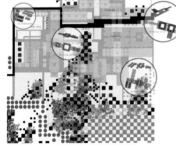

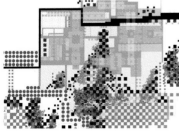

Rurban Settlement timeline

01 disused industrial territory is planted with forest vegetation in 10m x 10m squares

02 that creates a regular chess pattern

03 spontaneous growht deconstructs the regular pattern and creates a spatial framework of the settlement

04 infrastructure is built

05 transport access becomes a main public space artery

06 via on-line interface people choose their living units

07 houses consists of flexible modules - living units

08 housing responds to market demand

09 people occupy a settlement

10 new species occupy the forest edge

11 production forest and biomass patches are integrated within forest edge

12 housing builds up and create an interior - a climate envelope

13 in 50 years forest is harvested and new planted in place

DISPERSED TOWN - URBANIZED VILLAGE OR RURAL TOWN

Morozov Evgenie
Bazhenov Alexander

moroz_85@inbox.ru

Russian Federation

Ecological and technological scheme
Scheme of recycling waste and import resources

yard community

semi-recycling waste in yard community

partial export waste for city centers recycling

imports of electricity and water in yard management

citywide centers waste recycling

Over the centuries of towns' existence the form and the way of living of people practically have not changed. People still want to live in small houses and have a connection with nature, but use urban infrastructure. Megalopolises and rural settlements can not fully ensure these needs. So a small town, located near countryside and far from a megalopolis, but having good infrastructure communication with it, is the best form for society living in the near future. In addition towns, having a certain degree of autonomy, should complete a big city as a network of settlements, the structure of which makes it possible to maintain social and ecological balance of the whole agglomeration through self-regulating urban structures.

Urban self-regulation is carried out by reserve urban areas, which may get narrow, reaching a certain minimum, or expend, depending on the degree of development of a part of the town. Inside the reserve areas there are dispersed urban neighborhoods with a different functional dominant, which are able to expand and get narrow through them. This principle allows the city to change quickly and adapt to emergent new social, environmental and economic requirements. Environmental self-regulation of the town is monitoring the responsibility area of the city. To maintain the ecological balance between the natural and built environment at all stages of urban development we focus on the rational use of resources, increasing waste recycling within the city, in the spatial correlation between city and nature.

Environmental self-regulation at the neighborhood level is ensured through the establishment of semi-residential complexes of households managed by the community of residents. At this level,

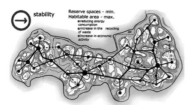

stability

Reserve spaces - min.
Habitable area - max.
● reducing energy consumption
● increase in the recycling of waste
● increase in economic activity

growth

Reserve spaces - decrease
Habitable area - increase
● max. amount of energy consumed
● min. recycling of waste
● decreasing the degree of economic activity

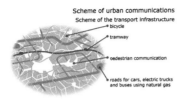

Scheme of urban communications
Scheme of the transport infrastructure
- bicycle
- tramway
- pedestrian communication
- roads for cars, electric trucks and buses using natural gas

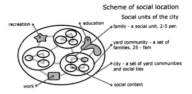

Scheme of social location
Social units of the city
- recreation
- education
- family - a social unit. 2-5 per.
- yard community - a set of families. 25 - fam
- city - a set of yard communities and social ties
- work
- social context

with the help of eco-technological device, semi-recycling of waste and water purification are carried out. As residential complexes develop and become more complex, communities begin to consume less citywide energy.

In the economic aspect self-regulating should be expressed in the flexibility of adaptive manufacturing systems. They should have the spatial opportunity to change their functional content according to requirements of today. At the same time in the areas of development and transformation it is necessary to maintain a socially and economically stable core around which functional complexes grow and get transformed. They can serve as major educational institutions, research laboratories, sports complexes, etc.

To create an active urban self-regulating system, social connections need to be promoted, through involving communities into the process of continuing transformation of urban structure, and realization of their creative potential.

Self-regulation of municipal bonds includes providing people with choice of vehicles, while the necessary condition is the orientation for environmentally-friendly transport, mainly public, completed with individual compact one.

The proposed location of a dispersed town is in an area of Moscow agglomeration, at a sufficient distance from Moscow (50 km). This place is included into the zone of Moscow economic expansion and has good infrastructural links with it. Similar areas are found near many big cities in the world, which, as cultural and economic centers, suffer from the megalopolis problems. The principles on which this project is based may be universal for creation of the balanced existence of the society in the 21st century and beyond.

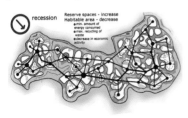

recession
Reserve spaces - increase
Habitable area - decrease
- min. amount of energy consumed
- max. recycling of waste
- decrease in economic activity

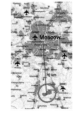

Moscow

70 km

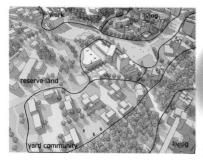

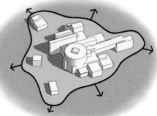

Production center - growth

increase in the area of spatial localization
decrease of the reserve

Production center - recession

increase in the area of spatial localization
decrease of reserve area

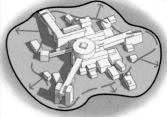

Production center - stability

max. area of spatial localization
min. area of a reserve area

Yard community - growht

Increase the degree of autonomy community
increase in the area of spatial localization
decrease of the reserve

Yard community - stability

Max. energy autonomy community
max. area of spatial localization
min. area of a reserve area

Yard community - recession

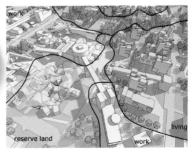

preservation of autonomy community
decrease in the area of spatial localization
increase in the area of the territory of the reserve

LIVING LANDSCAPES

URBAN GREEN

BIO INFRASTRUCTURES

ENERGY SYSTEMS

PARAMETRIC URBANISM

SOCIAL & COLLABORATIVE

THEORIES & STRATEGIES

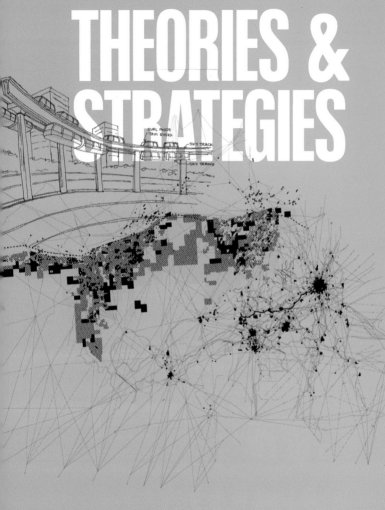

THEORIES &
STRATEGIES

LIVING LANDSCAPES

URBAN GREEN

BIO INFRASTRUCTURES

ENERGY SYSTEMS

PARAMETRIC URBANISM

SOCIAL & COLLABORATIVE

THEORIES & STRATEGIES

THEORIES & STRATEGIES

The projects in the 'Theories & Strategies' category envision a better future for humanity, and a more humane future for our cities. We are presented here with solutions and proposals that confront many of the inadequacies of past and current urban planning theory and practice.

The projects address the challenge of eradicating long-standing preconceptions which burden the decision-making process and render it rigid and thus incapable of adapting to unpredicted emergent needs, by means of revolutionary ideas that inevitably cause sociological mutations.

The effectiveness of the long-established top-down strategy of decision-making is often questioned on account of its inability to create sustainable cities for the future. The dominant theories of the last few hundred years have failed to include notions such as mutation and/or adaptation of space, use, density and socio-economics.

These innovative proposals create flexible systems from and with an entirely different viewpoint. In the quest for a self-sufficient city any design process with a controlled and pre-defined outcome is destined to fail. Only a dynamic self-generated and self-adapting system will be able to provide the conditions for resource optimization. Local decisions affect the whole, and the micro is just as important as the macro.

The means employed here is not the simple mimesis of nature's optimal closed energy systems but an astute interpretation of the canons that determine their functions.

Their goal is the efficient space and thus efficient resource distribution: in other words, economy (the disposition or regulation of the parts or functions of any organic whole; an organized system or method).

Axioms have no place in such dynamic systems: instead, a theory/strategy feedback loop is used to refine the methods and parameters of these organic design tools.

It is clear, however, that none of the envisioned systems could ever be conceived without a primary condition: an optimistic, collaborative society with strong links to nature.

We are not being asked to reminisce over romantic pre-industrial rural societies but to reflect on the bold decisions that we as a society will soon be asked to make, in order to change the social and economic structures that determine the way we build our cities.

LIVING LANDSCAPES

URBAN GREEN

BIO INFRASTRUCTURES

ENERGY SYSTEMS

PARAMETRIC URBANISM

SOCIAL & COLLABORATIVE

THEORIES & STRATEGIES

STRAND CITY

Stoner Jill
Ibone Santiago
Eduardo Pintos
jstoner@socrates.berkeley.edu

United States

This is not a utopian proposal. Its order emerges from within our existing cities, attaching itself to the linear infrastructures developed in the 20th century to support mobility—the freeways, autobahns, rondas, autostrads, turnpikes and M-roads that are very the lifelines of the contemporary metropolis. Formerly dedicated to speed and responsible for the enormous consumption of carbon resources, these sinuous tentacles that seem to choke our cities and separate them even from themselves can become, with the gradual obsolescence of the automobile, the loci of a new urban form. This form celebrates emptiness as well as density, proximity to air and wilderness as well as to each other. As for the patterns into which these strands are woven, each city's specific geography, ecology and culture will provoke its own, unique possibilities. What follows are suggestions for the coastal strand cities of San Francisco and Barcelona.

Strand cities are tall, dense and thin. They place us close to each other, to our social institutions, to the resources of fog, rain and wind, and to the respective landscapes of species diversity and productive agriculture. To one side of the strand: the wilderness, to the other: the farm. And high above the ground, the plats of San Francisco and patis of Barcelona form the finer strands of public space that weave themselves among the attenuated towers.

LIVING LANDSCAPES

URBAN GREEN

BIO INFRASTRUCTURES

ENERGY SYSTEMS

PARAMETRIC URBANISM

SOCIAL & COLLABORATIVE

THEORIES & STRATEGIES

LIVING LANDSCAPES

URBAN GREEN

BIG INFRASTRUCTURES

ENERGY SYSTEMS

PARAMETRIC URBANISM

SOCIAL & COLLABORATIVE

THEORIES & STRATEGIES

NEW BOSTON

Alexander Dixon

alexander.m.dixon@gmail.com

United States

2036 — ISOLATION

The suburban exodus was beginning to
peak, and in the wake of the thousands
who had already journeyed back into the
city of Boston vast tracts of housing and
infrastructure sat idle, slowly deteriorating. Gradually, fields of solar trackers
began to appear, reusing in reverse
fashion the existing electrical grid, and
tended by lone inhabitants who monitored
their efficiency in complete solitude. The
solar shepherds committed themselves
to three-year stints, a pseudo-monastic
period of eremitical reflection and
thought, gathering but once a year for
a single communion with their nearest
neighbors.
The antithesis of the city…

2044 — REINVENTION

The influx of families and, consequently,
businesses and commercial interests
from the suburbs strained Boston's
existing built environment, putting pressure on the city to increase housing and
office space. In an effort to avoid the
impending building crisis, the city, in an
unprecedented move, rezoned many of
the densest urban areas to accommodate
vertical expansion. Office buildings were
renovated into apartment complexes, and
the upper storeys of the tallest buildings
became lobbies for the new vertical
additions.
The dual city…

2053 — IMAGINATION

Travel became a leisure activity, and the city was returned to the pedestrian. The metropolis, sans voiture (carless). The 50s saw the beginning of what was to redefine the way individuals interacted with the urban environment. Architecture fused with communications technology, sociology and behavioral modeling under the umbrella of environmental design. There were no longer singular elements; the city was seen as an interpolating chronology of situations, events and responses. It was reactive, traversable, malleable and playful.
The interactive city…

LIVING LANDSCAPES

URBAN GREEN

BIO INFRASTRUCTURES

ENERGY SYSTEMS

PARAMETRIC URBANISM

SOCIAL & COLLABORATIVE

THEORIES & STRATEGIES

SIDERY

Carcamo Luis Manuel
Lizbeth Montejano
amasarte@yahoo.com.mx

Mexico

Quality of matter depends on the quality of consciousness

Man has now created a chaotic environment that manifests his inner state of mind. In this time, mankind has been generating an environment full of chaos which is nothing more than the manifestation of his particular state of mind.

The origin of suffering comes from ignorance of the true nature of reality which impels us to identify ourselves with mental patterns that give us a distorted view of who we are affecting our relationship with nature and with the others creating an environment of fear and distrust.

The city of the future requires our best in terms of technological solutions to preserve and restore our planet and its spices but in order to solve human problems we require solutions of conscience.

Our vision

If we want to create a healthy and constructive environment it is necessary to develop inner peace to generate a higher state of consciousness.

The relationship between man and the city is the same as the relationship between man with his inner self. We are constantly creating our own reality. When the city acts as a system forming a dynamic habitat, every action taken will produce a change in the units and the environment. The synergy or coordinated action produces an effect greater than the sum of individual effects. To achieve a well-integrated community, affinity is required in each of its parts whether natural or human environment

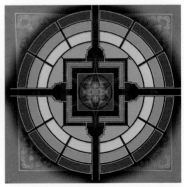

Our proposal

We believe that the city of the future must base its design in symbolic elements that represent the highest ideals of humanity by promoting and celebrating unity within diversity. Sideris is a model city that although it is planned in Mexico, it could developed anywhere in the world since it celebrates what unites us; the recognition of our common origin with every sentient being on earth and the universe.

Sideris represents the creation and expansion of the universe. The urban design revolves around a Unity Temple that we have called Sideris-Shakti which in sanskrit refers to the creative energy of the universe present in every one of us. Sideris-Shakti is an ecumenical temple that connects us with the purest expression of love by recognizing the power of creation which beats within the heart of every person.

Sideris City represents the underlying order of the universe that for millennia man has sensed and represented by the creation of extraordinary "mandalas" replete with symbolism and meaning.

The geometric pattern of the city is based on sacred geometry forms that constitute the energy matrix of nature. This is the purest expression of the beauty, product of the inscrutable cosmic intelligence that man has revered since the beginning of time.

We believe that applying these principles to the urban planning will contribute to the development of a highly synergistic society promoter of universal values that will become hallmarks of a new humanity.

THE CITY AS A MODEL OF THE EVOLUTIONARY PROCESS OF MAN TOWARDS ENLIGHTMENT

Universal Temple	SideriShakti (Sanctuary of the Self)
Main Square	Open space with the generator strokes of Sacred Geometry
Multicultural Centre	Museum of World Religions, Convention Centre & Educational Establishments
Devotional Centers	Private spaces for spiritual, religious and civil organizations
Green Areas	Parks, gardens, resting areas, sculptural spaces, etc.
Commercial Zone	Cultural Zone, Commercial, Services and Entertainment
Residential Area	Houses and condos that are linked to the rest of development

LIVING LANDSCAPES

URBAN GREEN

BIO INFRASTRUCTURES

ENERGY SYSTEMS

PARAMETRIC URBANISM

SOCIAL & COLLABORATIVE

THEORIES & STRATEGIES

SANTA MONICA ALGAE FARM BIO-ARCHITECTURE

Hui Christine

christinecarter765@msn.com

Hong Kong

Every living organism on Earth represents a perfectly functioning system, well adapted to the environment as a result of millions of years of evolution. The structure of these organisms can be developed into new dimensions in architecture and city planning.

The proposed scheme is located on the Santa Monica beach, Los Angeles. Los Angeles was the first city, which mentioned sustainability in the 1970s. However, over the last 30 years Los Angeles has suffered from high levels of air pollution, and is considered one of the most polluted cities in the US. Santa Monica beach is in a worse situation with water pollution levels hitting a near-record high in Los Angeles County. Thousands of vehicles emit huge amounts of carbon dioxide. Therefore, the conditions of the site and temperature create the best environment for algae growth and soothing the pollution issues in the area.

Algae are photosynthetic organisms; they vary from small single-celled forms to complex multi-cellular forms. They are regarded negatively by people and can be described as a dirty, nasty and smelly. Nevertheless, this small organism does play significant roles in air and water pollution.

The algae farm:
The algae farm is a self-sufficient building. The form is inspired by the algae nano-structure systems and the program of the farm consists of a café, laboratory, gallery, staff rooms, sauna rooms and a bath area. Three entrances haven been designed to meet the circulation requirements.

This design allows people to become more aware and understand the environmental issues concerned and addresses the importance of how people need to change in order to maintain a sustainable environment. My designs show an algae world for visitors who can observe the process of algae oil production. Human waste can also be utilized as the 'nutrient' of the algae. The by-products of algae (such as algae powder, clean water) are going to be used in the cosmetic bath, and will be pumped to taps around the building supplying drinking water for visitors. The algae fuel would be sold or be used in the farm.

The skin:
In my proposed design, the façade has two functions. Firstly, it provides the space for algae bloom and secondly, it creates an unpredictable ever-changing colour façade. The colours range from pale green to bright green; from bright green to brown; from brown to pink and white.

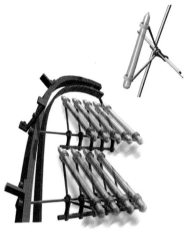

In order to increase the speed of the photosynthesis, the bioreactor is reduced in size. Smaller plastic tubes operate and inter-connect together; the bioreactor tubes cover the south and west façade. Each plastic tube connects to an international joint. By using the suns path data in Los Angeles, a central computer system is able to control the movement of the plastic tubes.

To produce fuel from CO_2, algae and other photosynthetic organism liquid will be pumped into a plastic photo-bioreactor and exposed to sunlight. The mass of algae can double or triple in size within 24 hours. During photosynthesis, carbon dioxide will be captured and converted into oxygen and biomass. Up to 99% of the carbon dioxide can be converted. The algal oil can then be converted into bio-diesel through a routine process called transesterification, in which it is processed using ethanol and a catalyst. Enzymes are then used to convert starches from the remaining bio-mass into sugars, which are fermented by yeasts to produce ethanol.

LIVING LANDSCAPES

URBAN GREEN

BIO INFRASTRUCTURES

ENERGY SYSTEMS

PARAMETRIC URBANISM

SOCIAL & COLLABORATIVE

THEORIES & STRATEGIES

0
1
2.5
5 m

LIVING LANDSCAPES

URBAN GREEN

BIO INFRASTRUCTURES

ENERGY SYSTEMS

PARAMETRIC URBANISM

SOCIAL & COLLABORATIVE

THEORIES & STRATEGIES

SEA FARM CITY – PROBLEM STATEMENT

Rush Richard D.

archestr88@comcast.net

United States

Like a station in space, each sea farm city will begin by constructing a basic sea farm living and working unit. The unit will include undersea fish farms (shown as spheres) working spaces for people, and dwelling spaces above them. Each sea farm living and working unit (sflawu) will be manufactured on land and assembled at sea. It will be anchored in place and include a helicopter pad for emergency access.

As the sea farm comunity grows and other sflawu's are built, key related building types will be constructed to provide service spaces, power, communications and community living and working spaces.

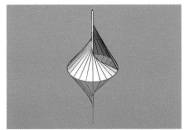

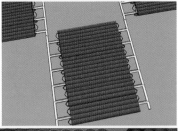

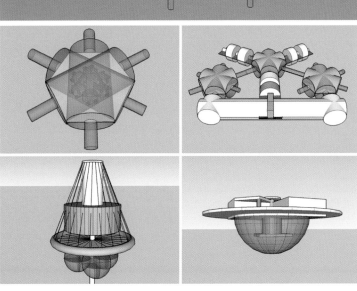

LIVING LANDSCAPES

URBAN GREEN

BIO INFRASTRUCTURES

ENERGY SYSTEMS

PARAMETRIC URBANISM

SOCIAL & COLLABORATIVE

THEORIES & STRATEGIES

385

A MODEL FOR THE RETURN TO SUS- TAINABLE CITY LIFE?

Lemos Antony

asileso@gmail.com

Portugal

Can the modern city cope with change? Or should future urbanists foresee the construction of new cities built from scratch? What is the future of today's urban centers? Is modern man capable or willing to put in the enormous amounts of energy required to change systems?

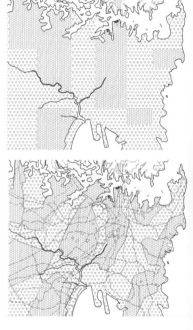

These are matters that should be at the forefront of mankind's thoughts. Great advances have been made in the direction I foresee. New hybrid buildings and a new craze in the architectural circle oriented at achieving green architecture. A lot of it is on a more modest scale, but the seeds of this vision are sprouting. New materials, other newly revived construction practices and maybe what is to me some of the most exciting work to date... unprecedented models in living as today's man not only gains sophistication but also ecological awareness. We already demand it in our houses, how long before it becomes priority in our cities?

Can we change?

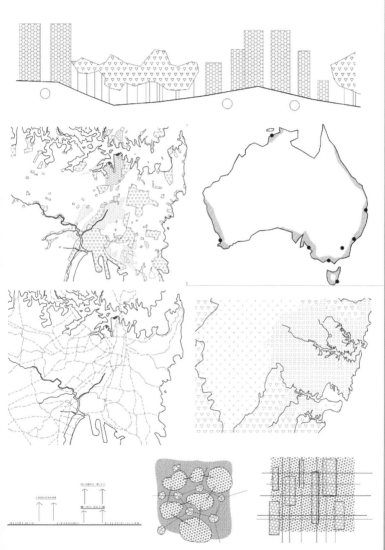

LIVING LANDSCAPES

URBAN GREEN

BIO-INFRASTRUCTURES

ENERGY SYSTEMS

PARAMETRIC URBANISM

SOCIAL & COLLABORATIVE

THEORIES & STRATEGIES

GREENING THE CITY, CONNECTING COMMUNITIES, C2C CITY

Giorgetti Clothilde
Duncan Crowley
Ignasi Cubi

clothildegio@yahoo.com

France

Greening the city, connecting communities, C2C Barcelona
Create urban greenway / CPUL mesh
Develop more bikeways/ walkways to easily connect from within city centre to nature: rivers, sea, surrounding hills. Allow all abandoned spaces to become indefinite temporary gardens. Specify strategic zones as permanent community gardens, including within all existing public parks and schools. Connect these nodes by greenways. Turn greenways into CPULS (Continuous Productive Urban Landscapes), Plant fruit and nut trees, berry hedges, diverse vegetation, food. These bio threads allow nature into the city; butterflies, song birds, pollen. Use city roofspace(s) as one vast CPUL, solar energy harvest, water collection zone and new Public Park. As private car use diminishes turn old "car lanes" into "food lanes". Create mixed use clusters around gardens, part of the urban fabric: play area, sport complex, café. Make spaces experimental, adaptable and open to everyone. Let all life adapt and grow.

Via Verde BCN: A series of greenway ripples, radiating out from the green heart of the city.

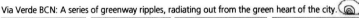

Images c/o Ronda Verda

DOKDO

Won Ho Sung
Yang Hyeonjeong
Lee Yulmi
Jung Minhyuk
dnjsthdnjs@hanmail.net

Republic of Korea

Yet, there are lots of elements that peril
the peace between the countries in the
world. Among these ones, the one issue
is the opposition between the countries
over the international dispute area.
These areas usually have the high economic and natural value, so now Japan is
claiming Dokdo islet is Japan's territory,
that is to say, this small islet is gathering
as international conflict.

This project is to design the point of
peace for solving dispute in the international conflict area and the new conceptual marine city having self-sufficient
ability area aquatic leisure facilities. This
planning will be new multi-functional city
developing energy and natural resources
as specialized area.

Finally, Dokdo's planning will be able to
the sustainable development.

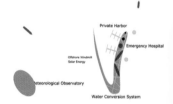

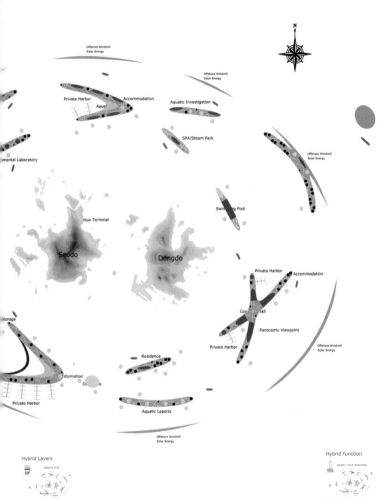

Offshore Windmill
Solar Energy

Offshore Windmill
Solar Energy

Private Harbor   Accommodation   Aquatic Investigation
Aqua...

SPA/Steam Park

...mental Laboratory

Offshore Windmill
Solar Energy

...rbus Terminal

Swimming Pool

Seodo   Dongdo

Private Harbor   Accommodation

...torage   Co... ...all

Panoramic Viewpoint

Private Harbor

...formation   Residence   Offshore Windmill
                                        Solar Energy

...ormation
D... ...e

Private Harbor   Aquatic Leports

Offshore Windmill
Solar Energy

Hybrid Layers
Leisure Line

Leisure Layer
Commercial Line   Energy Line   Hybrid scape

Commercial Layer   Energy Layer

Hybrid function
Aquatic Culture_Waterscape

Aquatic culture
Innovative Culture_High Technology

Ecological Culture_Green Area

Innovative culture   Ecological culture

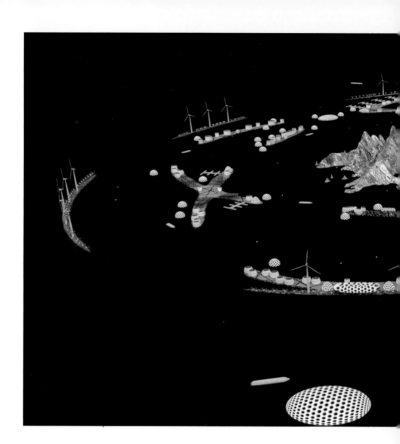

LIVING LANDSCAPES

URBAN GREEN

BIO INFRASTRUCTURES

ENERGY SYSTEMS

PARAMETRIC URBANISM

SOCIAL & COLLABORATIVE

THEORIES & STRATEGIES

NEW URBAN ECONOMIES

Lloyd Jordan J.

jordan.lloyd@gmail.com

United Kingdom

New Urban Economies

In 2007, the UN announced that more than 50% of the world's population now resides in cities. New Urban Economies considers the design of cities through the infrastructures that feed them. Therefore, cities should be looked at not as static objects on a map, but as the ever changing systems that they actually are. Understanding cities as complex ecologies and designing them to follow the same closed system ecologies of nature will be a step toward a truly self sufficient city.

Self sufficient cities must engage with the fundamental building blocks of their continued existence: its economy, its industry and its communities. These are complex systems unto themselves. It is possible to reconfigure existing systems we take for granted, such as food production/distribution and waste processing into self sufficient economies that can sustain the cities of tomorrow as a closed loop system for the benefit of all.

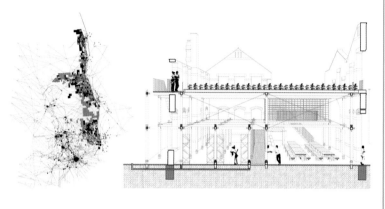

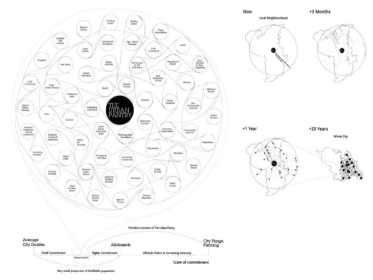

Possible outcome of The Urban Pantry

Average City Dweller

Small Commitment

Allotments

Higher Commitment

City Fringe Farming

Lifestyle choice or increasing necessity

Scale of commitment

Very small proportion of Sheffield's population

LIVING LANDSCAPES

URBAN GREEN

BIO INFRASTRUCTURES

ENERGY SYSTEMS

PARAMETRIC URBANISM

SOCIAL & COLLABORATIVE

THEORIES & STRATEGIES

A VISION FOR TRIVANDRUM 2035 AD

Conil Jos

josconil@yahoo.com

India

Trivandrum, the capital of the Indian state of Kerala, is an emerging IT and higher education hub of South India. As with most Indian cities, Trivandrum is affected by infrastructure bottlenecks, environmental degradation and has a rich heritage to preserve.

This design proposal is an endeavour to address these issues with a futuristic vision for the year 2035 AD.

The objectives of this proposal are Sustainable Transportation, Energy, Water Supply, Fuel & Waste management; Mixed use planning and preservation of heritage. The planning concepts and design elements are as follows:

An inner, intermediate and outer loop roads for the existing city and new urban modules which are large car free premises, planned beyond the inner loop road. These loop roads and Urban modules employ new technologies like Sky Track Integrated Metro system; Shell & Core smart cars and Intelligent Roadways.

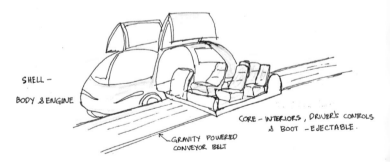

SHELL –
BODY & ENGINE

CORE – INTERIORS, DRIVER'S CONTROLS & BOOT – EJECTABLE.

GRAVITY POWERED CONVEYOR BELT

THE SHELL & CORE SMART CAR.

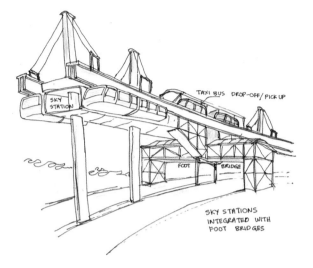

TAXI BUS DROP-OFF/PICK UP

SKY STATION

FOOT BRIDGE

SKY STATIONS
INTEGRATED WITH
FOOT BRIDGES

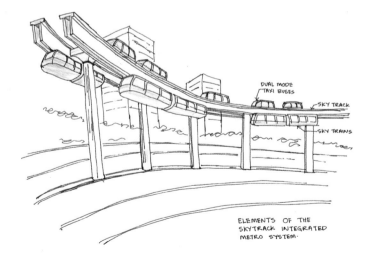

DUAL MODE
TAXI BUSES

SKY TRACK

SKY TRAINS

ELEMENTS OF THE
SKYTRACK INTEGRATED
METRO SYSTEM.

LIVING SYSTEM

Monfort Leon Maria Celia
Guillermo Aloy Bibiloni
Ekain Olaizola Lizarralde

mariacelia.monfort@gmail.com

Spain

We saw a chance in this competition of trying to think how could be a new city in this century, how to use the sostenibility as a main tool of designing urbanism and architecture , how to develop the self sufficient city. Just taking a look arround us, we can see the boom of the new cities in xina. The impact of china´s growing throught the configuration of new cities which sacrificies original and historic identities in order to serve productive logics, with their baggage of destruction, change and imitation, serves to eximplify a emergence of finding a new urban refer-ence in this ever interconnected world in which cities are presented stripped of their history.

But, what´s happening in asia, around xina? Other countries are trying to copy this model. Vietnam, a country with still empty areas, wonderfull landscapes and quite poor, is being recovered economi-cally thanks to the tourism. This is why they are thinking about creating new cities mainly touristic. This is the case of phan tieth, in the south coast of the region of na trang. That´s a big challenge to project a new city, which we have decided be based in a system but with own identity, somehow the system has to generate identity.

ANALYSIS OF GREEN AREAS 1/60 000

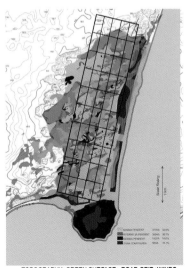

**TOPOGRAPHY+GREEN SURFACE+ ROAD GRID+WINDS
1/60 000**

ANALYSIS OF TOPOGRAPHY 1/60 000

TERRITORIAL AND LOCAL WINDS CITY S ROAD GRID 1/60 000

ADAPTED ROAD GRID TO TOPOGRAPHY AND
GREEN SURFACE 1/60 000

NOT BUILT ZONES FOR TOPOGRAPHY AND GREEN SURFACE
1/60 000

LIVING LANDSCAPES

URBAN GREEN

BIO INFRASTRUCTURES

ENERGY SYSTEMS

PARAMETRIC URBANISM

SOCIAL & COLLABORATIVE

THEORIES & STRATEGIES

LIVING LANDSCAPES

URBAN GREEN

BIO INFRASTRUCTURES

ENERGY SYSTEMS

PARAMETRIC URBANISM

SOCIAL & COLLABORATIVE

THEORIES & STRATEGIES

SYNERGETIC SYSTEM

Bataev Maxim

maximbataev@mail.com

Russian Federation

The project doesn't presuppose the solution of city's space, but rather methods and system of its development. Self-organization means the degree of freedom in the structure, that based on synergetic principles. The main aim of this town-planning project is creation of the genetic code of an universal matrix, which isn't oriented on subjective and perpetually changeable city's reality. It is just a symbolic model of the universe.
Synergetic principles of the project.
Homeostasis
Every system has its own aim of existence. The idea of this project is to include a human life spontaneity and an irrational social phenomena in the process of projection to turn them into the unity of variety. The system is flexible and integral.
Not closed
The structure of the city is changeable in time. At the same time it is finished and ready for further development. Ideal city of the 21st century is open and will never stop its growth. "We need system, which can flexibly react to changes. When I speak about the general plan I mean general system"(Kishyo Kurokava).
This solution requires an uniformity and equivalence of unity parts in the project. The city is homogeneous on horizontal.
Hierarchy
Hierarchy is one of the determinative order principle of the universe. Horizontal hierarchy of classical city is democratic, on the other side it contains inertia of development and forced self- regulation. After one moment the city forms in disorder, which isn't possible to stop.
There is a horizontal zoning in this project, but the main functions are served along the vertical axis. An importance is predetermined by structure.
A general plan realization amounts to 20-30 percent, other 70-80 percents are dictated by our life and its abruptness. Synergetic system gives opportunity to include chaos in the process of projection as a variety of unity.

Structural scheme

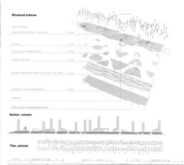

Section. scheme

Plan. scheme

SYNERGETICsystem

LIVING LANDSCAPES

URBAN GREEN

BIO INFRASTRUCTURES

ENERGY SYSTEMS

PARAMETRIC URBANISM

SOCIAL & COLLABORATIVE

THEORIES & STRATEGIES

LIVING LANDSCAPES

URBAN GREEN

BIO-INFRASTRUCTURES

ENERGY SYSTEMS

PARAMETRIC URBANISM

SOCIAL & COLLABORATIVE

THEORIES & STRATEGIES

SELF-SUFFICIENT CITY COPENHAGEN

Jensen Thomas
Thomas T

ttj@sum-things.com

Denmark

The over-all premise for this project is
the idea that space does not have to be
pre-determined in terms of type and
function. Rather, by generating a multitude
of conditions (spatial and formal qualities) a space will be inhabited and put to
use according to its spatial and formal
characteristics. This project disregards
the notion of fixed typologies (and their
implied spatial configurations) and
focuses on qualities and characteristics
of space and form. The self-suffucient
CITY investigates the bottom-up
morphogenetic (and morphodynamic)
processes which generate differentiated
characteristics in space and form. This
focus means that architects, as designers, loose control over what emerges
in the end. Control is, instead, executed
on a different level of the process (see
'Scripting' below). By coding the system
according to organisational and spatial
intentions and determining behavior and
performance designers design a mode of
operation, or the process, rather than
a city or the buildings within the city.

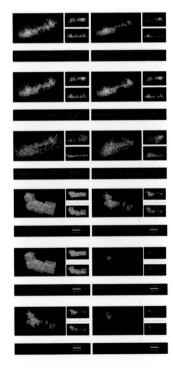

city aerial

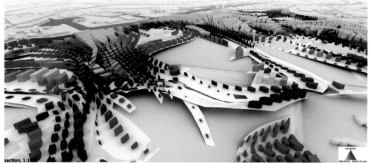

section, 1:1...

sample site aerial

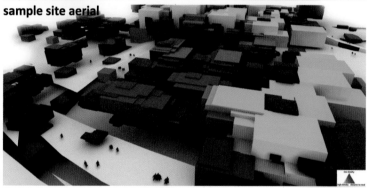

sample site street view

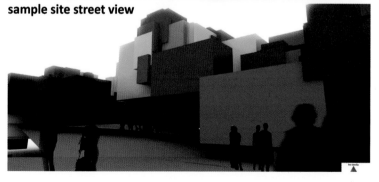

low density

high density   distance to road

LIVING LANDSCAPES

URBAN GREEN

BIO-INFRASTRUCTURES

ENERGY SYSTEMS

PARAMETRIC URBANISM

SOCIAL & COLLABORATIVE

THEORIES & STRATEGIES

ECO SIN COMPENSATOR

Schifferdecker Uli

Uli.Schifferdecker@gmx.de

Germany

Sustainibility fights global warming in a passiv way. While we think about zero energy housing billions of people think about getting a car and air conditioner. We need to fight global warming on a different level. We need to do something against it and not just slowing down the process. The Eco Sin Compensator is the first project introduced to the world which actually cools down the planet, which humanity heated up since industrialisation. It is compensting our ecological sins. As a side effect it produces energy which we use for dwelling.

Location.The northern hemisphere is covererd by permafrost shrinking year to year. it´s not only responsible to protect us from global warming by cooling down the planet, it also contains huge amounts of methan which would be relaesed when it continues melting. It reaches down 20m to 300m, in summer it melts several meters on top.

Strategy. geothermy makes it possible to keep a constant temperature in buildings. in winter the cold air is exchanged by natural heat from the underground.

The Eco Sin Compensator does the same: in winter it brings the cold, up to -60°C into the permafrost to thicken it, in summer it`s strengthen and will melt less. each winter the process will be repeated: each year the amount of permfrost will grow to stabilize the world climate. A temperature difference more than -/+30°C can be used to gain energy in a temperature difference circuit generator. In winter -60°C in the atmosphere and little below 0°C in permafrost makes it possible provide enough energy for dwelling through out the winter.

By collecting biomass over the summer, which turnes into warm gas and expands in winter, antennas rise and pneumatic fabric encloses the settlement. in summer the cover folds back into the ground and the gas is used to produce energy for farming. in that way a comfortable life is provided, while permafrost increases. Now whole year farming is possible for self-sufficent living in the hardly accessseble north. I understand it as a new seed for living responsible in an enviroment which was before hard to cultivate.

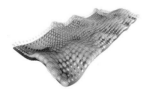

LIVING LANDSCAPES

URBAN GREEN

BIO INFRASTRUCTURES

ENERGY SYSTEMS

PARAMETRIC URBANISM

SOCIAL & COLLABORATIVE

THEORIES & STRATEGIES

LIVING LANDSCAPES

URBAN GREEN

BIO INFRASTRUCTURES

ENERGY SYSTEMS

PARAMETRIC URBANISM

SOCIAL & COLLABORATIVE

THEORIES & STRATEGIES

Iaac
Institute for
advanced
architecture
of Catalonia

IaaC
Institute for advanced architecture of Catalonia
C/Pujades 102 baixos, Poble Nou Barcelona 08005, Spain
T. (+34) 93 3209520
F. (+34) 93 3004333
info@iaac.net
www.iaac.net

Actar
Roca i Batlle, 2
08023 Barcelona, Spain
T. (+34) 93 4187759
F. (+34) 93 4186707
www.actar.com

CREDITS

3RD ADVANCED ARCHITECTURE CONTEST

Director
Lucas Cappelli

Coordinator
Marie Jacquinet

Contents Advisers
Willy Müller
Josep Mias
Haakon Karlsen jr.
Silvia Brandi
Tomas Diez

Communication Events
Jorge Ledesma
Mateo Lima Valente

Web Design
www.nitropix.com
Roxana Degiovanni
Agostina Cappelli

Web Developer
Emilio Degiovanni

Collaborators
Gawel Tyrala
Asli Aydin
Daria Bychkova
Nasreen Al Tamimi
Mohamed Omer
Florise Pages

Official Sponsor
HP - Hewlett-Packard
David Belles

Jury Members
Jaime Lerner
Architect, former Mayor of Curitiba, former President of UIA,
Mr. Mityrev
Representative for the Governor of Saint Petersburg,
Brett Steele
Director of the Architectural Association, London
Stan T. Allen
Dean of Princeton University School of Architecture
Yung Ho Chang
Head of the MIT Department of Architecture
Aaron Betsky
Director of The Cincinnati Art Museum
Haakon Karlsen Jr
Director of MIT Fab Lab Norway
Pankaj Joshi
Director of Urbanism Design Research Institute. Mumbai, India
Benyam Ali
Head of the Addis Ababa University Department of Architecture
JM Lin,
Architect , The Observer Design Group, Taipei, Taiwan
Bostian Vuga
Sadar & Vuga architects, Lubjana , Slovenia
Michel Rojkind
Rojkind Arquitecto, México
Vicente Guallart
Director of IAAC, Barcelona
Willy Müller,
Director of IAAC Development
Marta Malé-Alemany
Co-director of IAAC Master in Advanced Architecture
Areti Markopoulou
Academic Coordinator of IAAC Master in Advanced Architecture
Lucas Cappelli
Director of 3rd Advanced Architecture Contest

COLLABORATORS

Published by
IaaC – Institute for Advanced Architecture of Catalonia
Actar

Edited by
Lucas Cappelli
Vicente Guallart

Classification Introductions
Bio Infrastructure. Silvia Brandi
Energy Systems. Areti Nikolopoulou
Living Landscapes. Luciana Asinari
Parametric Urbanism. Areti Markopoulou
Social and Collaborative. Tomas Diez Ladera.
Theories and Strategies. Orfeas Giannakidis.
Urban Green. Vagia Pandou

Translation
Graham A. Thomson

Graphic Design
Actar Birkhäuser Pro

Collaborator
Monica Wittig

Printing
Ingoprint

Distribution
Actar Birkhäuser Distribution
Roca i Batlle 2
08023 Barcelona
T. (+34) 93 417 4 993
F. (+34) 93 418 6 707

ISBN 978-84-92861-33-0
DL B-24065-2010

Printed and bound in the European Union